Virgil *Aeneid* II

The following titles are available from Bloomsbury for the OCR specifications in Latin and Greek for examinations from June 2024 to June 2026

Cicero *Pro Caelio*: A Selection, with introduction, commentary notes and vocabulary by Georgina Longley

Juvenal *Satires*: A Selection, with introduction, commentary notes and vocabulary by John Godwin

Ovid *Fasti*: A Selection, with introduction, commentary notes and vocabulary by Robert Cromarty

Letters of Pliny: A Selection, with introduction, commentary notes and vocabulary by Carl Hope

Tacitus *Annals* XII: A Selection, with introduction, commentary notes and vocabulary by Simon Allcock

Tacitus *Annals* XIV: A Selection, with introduction, commentary notes and vocabulary by John Storey

Virgil *Aeneid* II: A Selection, with introduction, commentary notes and vocabulary by Dominic Jones

OCR Anthology for Classical Greek GCSE, covering the prescribed texts by Euripides, Herodotus, Homer and Xenophon, with introduction, commentary notes and vocabulary by Judith Affleck and Clive Letchford

OCR Anthology for Classical Greek AS and A Level, covering the prescribed texts by Aristophanes, Euripides, Herodotus, Homer, Plato and Plutarch, with introduction, commentary notes and vocabulary by Sam Baddeley, Benedict Gravell, Charlie Paterson, Neil Treble, Stuart R. Thomson and Chris Tudor

Online resources to accompany this book are available at bloomsbury.pub/OCR-editions-2024-2026. If you experience any problems, please contact Bloomsbury at onlineresources@bloomsbury.com

Virgil *Aeneid* II: A Selection

Lines 40–249, 268–317, 370–558

With introduction, commentary notes and vocabulary by Dominic Jones

BLOOMSBURY ACADEMIC

LONDON · NEW YORK · OXFORD · NEW DELHI · SYDNEY

BLOOMSBURY ACADEMIC
Bloomsbury Publishing Plc
50 Bedford Square, London, WC1B 3DP, UK
1385 Broadway, New York, NY 10018, USA
29 Earlsfort Terrace, Dublin 2, Ireland

BLOOMSBURY, BLOOMSBURY ACADEMIC and the Diana logo are
trademarks of Bloomsbury Publishing Plc

First published in Great Britain 2023

Cover image: Ranko Maras / Alamy Stock Photo

A catalogue record for this book is available from the British Library.

A catalog record for this book is available from the Library of Congress.

ISBN: PB: 978-1-3501-5647-0
       ePDF: 978-1-3501-5649-4
       eBook: 978-1-3501-5648-7

Typeset by RefineCatch Limited, Bungay, Suffolk
Printed and bound in India

To find out more about our authors and books visit www.bloomsbury.com
and sign up for our newsletters.

Contents

Preface

The text and notes found in this volume are designed to help any student of Latin who has conquered the language as far as GCSE and wishes to tackle parts of Book II of Virgil's *Aeneid* in the original.

The edition is, however, designed especially to guide those students who are reading Virgil's text in preparation for OCR's A Level Latin examination in 2025 and 2026. This includes AS Level students, who will focus on the book's first third (lines 40–249), and those selecting *Aeneid* II only as their Group 1 prescription.

The second book of Virgil's epic has never wanted for attention. It was the first book to receive an English verse translation, courtesy of Henry Howard, the Earl of Surrey, in 1557, and it has remained, almost ever since, one of the best known and most anthologized portions of the poem. The introduction to this volume aims to give readers a sense of what characterizes *Aeneid* II, and how its thematic concerns connect to the whole poem and the arc of Aeneas, as well as the text's original context.

There is also guidance on how to interrogate the poem at close quarters, what is known as 'practical criticism'. This part of the introduction trades more in questions than answers, on the rationale that students produce the most meaningful analysis when they are encouraged to pose questions for themselves. As a complement to this, the companion website contains two worked analyses of extracts from both the AS and A Level prescribed sections of Book II. There you will also find further information on the Helen/Venus episode; some additional detail on Virgil's metre; and some exemplar A Level (Section C) essay questions.

The commentary notes should help students pick through Virgil's Latin, with the spotlight on those gritty bits of poetic grammar and syntax which a post-GCSE language course will necessarily omit. The vocabulary at the back of this edition glosses every word in the prescribed lines, including those which belong to the AS Defined Vocabulary List.

Lastly, some acknowledgments. This volume would be significantly slighter and less scholarly were it not for two modern commentaries, those of Roland Austin (1964) and Nicholas Horsfall (2008). I am very grateful to the library of Horsfall's *alma mater*, Westminster School, for loaning me his (not inexpensive) commentary along with various other Virgil books, most of which have been overdue for about two years. I also owe an unpayable debt to past teachers and colleagues, to my parents, to Freyja and Nico: thank you.

Dominic Jones
Birmingham
January 2022

Introduction

The *Aeneid*

The *Aeneid* is an epic poem which tells how a prince of Troy, Aeneas, flees the sack of his city and sets out to found a new race – the Roman race – in central Italy. It is a mythological epic: Aeneas' mission is required by Fate and enforced by Jupiter, king of the gods. But in return for Aeneas' hardship, his descendants will one day achieve a very historical outcome: the glory of Rome's empire.

The poem was composed between 29 and 19 BC, when Virgil died, and it is the masterpiece of a poet hailed in his own lifetime, and ever since, as Rome's greatest. One reason the *Aeneid* has endured for 2,000 years is that it reaches beyond the foundation myth of Rome and poses universal questions about our relationship to the past and the future; the purpose of war; the struggle for self-mastery; the value of companionship; and what happens when individual and collective aims compete.

Virgil and Augustus

Publius Vergilius Maro ('Virgil') was born in 70 BC during the turbulent years of the late Republic. Between the poet's birth and his death in 19 BC, Rome endured twenty-nine years of war, sixteen of which were civil war. It was a lifetime which witnessed crisis and upheaval in politics, society, the economy and in the public conscience. This was the backdrop of Virgil's first forty years, but in 31 BC the decisive victory of Octavian over Mark Antony at Actium heralded a new regime and the prospect of stability for the war-weary Roman

Empire. Virgil never held political or military office, but his life and his career were profoundly shaped by the tumult of the late Republic and the first years of the early Empire.

Our poet was born to a family of farmers in the Po valley of northern Italy. His village lay close to Mantua in Cisalpine Gaul ('Gaul on this side of the Alps'), a province of Rome which spoke Latin but only received Roman citizenship in 49 BC, courtesy of Julius Caesar. Virgil was twenty-one at the time, and his education had taken him from Cremona to Milan and on to Rome, where an ambitious provincial might further himself through public speaking. It was not rhetoric but Greek and literature which captured Virgil's interest, however, and by the late 40s he was working on his first major work, the *Eclogues*.

The *Eclogues*, published around 37 BC, is a collection of ten poems modelled on the pastoral poems of the third-century Greek poet Theocritus. Each poem takes a dramatic form in which simple shepherds, using refined language, address themselves or each other on a range of themes, some more Theocritan (love, beauty, art), others more Virgilian (loss, upheaval, identity). The *Eclogues* handle complex material subtly and skilfully, and Virgil's engagement with a more marginal Greek poet established his status and attracted a powerful new patron, Gaius Cilnius Maecenas.

Maecenas was an aristocrat and a close associate of Augustus, the name Octavian took for himself in 27 BC. After the Battle of Actium, Augustus set to work carefully entrenching his regime, and like many dictators, he understood the soft power of art. Maecenas was appointed to nurture a generation of writers who might contribute to the brand-building exercise that accompanied the political revolution. Virgil's second major production, the *Georgics*, appeared in 29 BC with a dedication to Maecenas his patron, and Augustus figures prominently throughout the poem, although never by name.

The *Georgics* is longer and more obviously unified than the *Eclogues*. It is a single poem, some 2,000 lines, divided into four books which contain guidance on how to farm crops and livestock in Italy. This is didactic poetry, verse which instructs the reader. The poem contains quite technical guidance on issues like inspecting soil or managing a bee hive, knowledge picked up from a childhood in northern Italy and, later, from Campania where Virgil settled in the 30s. But the seemingly apolitical and timeless content conceals, not far beneath the surface, very contemporary concerns about the social and moral regeneration of Rome and its territories post-war. The *Georgics* reflects on the anxiety and hope felt by Romans as they processed their recent past and looked forward to the future: what values should they carry forward from the Republic, and what might that look like on a national, local and personal level? There is patriotism in the *Georgics* as well as direct praise of Augustus, but it is neither naïve nor unambiguous.

The Italian peninsula had been ravaged by war both directly, as a battleground, and indirectly, as property and rights were removed from communities which had backed the wrong side in wars. Mantua in Cisalpine Gaul was one such community forced to give up land to civil war veterans, and it is likely that Virgil's own family farm suffered in the resettlement process. This is the suggestion of his fourth-century commentator, Aelius Donatus, who records a land dispute settled in Virgil's favour only through the intervention of Maecenas (*Vita* 20). High-profile poets like Virgil, and his rough contemporaries Horace and Ovid, now relied on the goodwill of the imperial court for financial and professional security. Virgil's early career success will have brought pressure, even before Actium, for a more substantial engagement with the Augustan revolution, and at the halfway point of the *Georgics* we are told, 'Soon I will ready myself to relay the blazing battles of Caesar Augustus, and carry forward his name in glory for as many years as separate him from the very birth of Dawn' (III.46–8). Virgil turned to the epic genre, and the *Aeneid* is his large-scale response to the problems and prospects of the Augustan age.

It was the final undertaking of a tripartite career and, at nearly 10,000 lines, absorbed Virgil from 29 BC until his death ten years later. The poem was acclaimed well before it was published: the poet Propertius hailed it as 'something greater than the *Iliad*' (II.34.66) already in the mid-20s, and within Virgil's lifetime it was taught in Roman classrooms. Augustus took a keen interest, writing to Virgil regularly, and Donatus tells us that the poet personally recited Books II, IV and VI to his patron (*Vita* 32). When Virgil died at Brundisium in 19 BC, in the emperor's entourage, the poem was still due its final touches, and Virgil allegedly asked his executors to destroy the manuscript upon his death. Augustus countermanded the request, and the *Aeneid* became an instant classic.

Virgil and the epic genre

With each of his three works, Virgil graduated progressively in scale and subject, beginning with the episodic *Eclogues* (the longest being 111 lines) and culminating in the *Aeneid*, an epic in twelve books which spans a massive temporal and geographical range. The epic form was also in prestige terms the pinnacle of Latin literary forms, for three reasons: the weight of its subject matter; the form's technical demands; and the colossal status of Homer's *Iliad* and *Odyssey*. Classical epic is interested in states of order and disorder, human and divine, and the tensions which exist between those states. This includes how we relate to one another, how we relate to the past and the future, and how we respond to the fact of our mortality. Such profound subject matter requires a proportionate scope. Consider, at a glance, how much happens in the twelve books (9,896 lines) of Virgil's *Aeneid*:

The goddess Juno inflicts a storm on Aeneas' fleet. Jupiter intervenes and unveils Rome's destiny. Aeneas lands at Carthage (Book I). Aeneas tells the local queen, Dido, how the Trojans were tricked by the Wooden Horse; the city was torched and he narrowly escaped (Book II). He describes seven years of sailing the Mediterranean in search of a new home – first in Greece, then in Sicily (Book III). Back in Carthage, he wins the heart of Dido, then abandons her (Book IV). He returns to Sicily where he holds competitions in honour of his dead father (Book V). Next, he reaches Italy where he visits various figures in the Underworld (Book VI). He sails on to the mouth of the Tiber in central Italy, the region he is destined to settle. He meets opposition: several Italian tribes declare war on the Trojans (Book VII). Aeneas travels to the future site of Rome in order to make an alliance (Book VIII). His camp comes under siege in his absence and two Trojans try to send a message (Book IX). Fighting then rages between Aeneas' army and the locals, led by a warrior called Turnus (Book X). The slaughter continues, with tragic losses on both sides (Book XI). Eventually comes the showdown between Aeneas and Turnus. The latter is overpowered, and the war ends with his death (Book XII).

The task of organizing such diverse material required a deft touch, one skilled at varying pace, place, tone and content, balancing the ratio of narration to description to direct speech, and unifying its structure.

Virgil was also writing in the shadow of Homer and Ennius, who in the second century was the first to adapt Homer's dactylic hexameter to Latin epic verse. Homer's epics emerged from a long oral tradition; the *Aeneid*, like Ennius' *Annales*, belonged to a literate culture, in which the poet had ready access to earlier texts, both Greek and Roman. From the 600-odd lines of Ennius which have survived, we know that he imported from Homer certain elements which are visible all over the *Aeneid*: the extended simile, the *ecphrasis* (a verbal visualizing of a poignant object or scene), the *aristeia* (a hero's mid-battle killing spree), extensive direct speech, and gods appearing in person to mortals. Virgil also took from Ennius a chronological compass which connected the heroic age of Greece to the historical age of contemporary Rome.

'Roman history in the future tense' was W. H. Auden's critique of the *Aeneid*, and it is true that Virgil's epic looks to the past for its positive vision of the future. The poem takes its subject, Aeneas, from the Homeric world, but the legend of his flight from Troy and arrival in Latium, creating a part-Trojan, part-Italian race, was sufficiently well known and sufficiently patriotic for an Augustan audience. The semi-historical status of Aeneas also gave Virgil flexibility to mould his protagonist in light of contemporary Roman values. Moreover, through the son of Aeneas, Iulus (also called Ascanius), Virgil could trace descent from the first Roman down to the Iulii, the aristocratic family to which Augustus belonged.

This splicing of the mythological and the historical was not new or noteworthy in Latin epic poetry. Gnaeus Naevius in the third century wrote an epic which began with Aeneas and ended with the first war between Rome and Carthage (264–241 BC). His younger contemporary, Ennius, took Rome's story from the fall of Troy down to 184 BC. In Virgil's lifetime, Varro Attacinus wrote an epic celebrating Caesar's campaign in Gaul, and Cicero wrote two epic poems, both lost, on his own political career in the late Republic. Virgil's *Aeneid* belongs to a tradition, therefore, of enlarging and fictionalizing historical narratives, a tradition which continued into the first century AD with works like Silius' *Punica* and Lucan's *Pharsalia*.

In 29 BC, however, when Virgil began his poem, Rome stood at a palpable turning point in history. Around this same time, the historian Livy embarked on his vast history of Rome, *Ab Urbe Condita*, and both works seek to affirm Rome's heroic origins and adumbrate Augustan values. The two texts share more than their sweeping scope. Both treat the *urbs capta* motif early in their respective works: Livy in his first book, Virgil in Book II of the *Aeneid*. A contemporary Roman reading Livy's sack of Alba (I.29) or Virgil's sack of Troy might have recognized in the background Caesar's siege of Massilia in 49 BC, where a testudo-ram similar to the Greeks' (441n.) was deployed (*De Bello Civili* II.2). Virgil's military lexicon (47, 265, 442) and technological anachronisms (492) evoke civil war episodes like Mark Antony's siege of Mutina in 43 BC more obviously than Homer's *Iliad*. Other elements in Book II of the *Aeneid*, such as the clanging of weapons (303), spreading flames (289) and the abduction of women (403), are common to Livy's accounts of sacked cities, and it is possible both he and Virgil were drawing on an earlier treatment of the *urbs capta* in Ennius' *Annales*.

The fall of Troy in *Aeneid* II signifies more than the stimulus for Aeneas' journey. It represents the sudden upheaval of a once-thriving community following a hard siege, and in historical terms Troy symbolizes the ruin which must precede renewal. King Priam is the embodiment of Troy, and so his death – one of the climaxes of *Aeneid* II – is charged with symbolic and historical significance. Aeneas' epitaph for Priam (554–8) recalls Cassius Dio's judgement on the shoreside murder of Pompey, Caesar's civil war opponent, in 48 BC (42.5.3). Each man had wielded vast power in the eastern Mediterranean; each was beheaded pathetically on a shoreline; and each death was a historical watershed. There is even historical resonance, some have claimed, in Virgil's choice of *ingens* for Priam's corpse, evoking Pompey's *cognomen*, *Magnus* (557n.). Such hints of historical irony are important but they should not outweigh our appreciation of the poem as, primarily, a work of literature.

The status of Aeneas

It is possible to interpret Aeneas reductively as little more than the avatar of Augustus: just as Aeneas imposed order on the world by founding the Roman race, so will Augustus unify the Roman state and bring stability to its empire. Moments in the *Aeneid* are passionately patriotic, especially the explicit references to Augustus in prophecy scenes (Jupiter in Book I, the parade of heroes in Book VI, and the shield of Aeneas in Book VIII). But to dismiss the *Aeneid* as elegant propaganda is to deny the poem its complexity and nuance. The poem confronts the human cost of empire throughout, and in many ways the poem's casualties, such as Dido and Turnus, are more emotionally engaging characters. Moreover, the glimpses we get of 'Roman history in the future tense' are contingent on Aeneas and his descendants persevering with productive values and resisting their antithesis. Aeneas' political identity derives from his moral identity.

The poem's presiding positive value is *pietas*, an unswerving commitment to what a Roman male would deem worthy: gods (personal and public), the Roman state and the patriarchal family unit. These three elements, in the Augustan ideology, mutually reinforce one another. The term *pietas* rejects the sort of egotism visible in the late-Republic's clash of magnates, and the suggestion of the *Aeneid* is that Rome's future greatness requires the subordination of individual to collective interests: the suppression of impulsive, individualist *furor* and the promotion of pro-social *pietas*. This is evident in Book II, especially in the desperate skirmishing of Aeneas and his followers after the visit of Hector's ghost. Forms of *furo*, and its cousin *ardeo* (lit. 'I burn'), appear seven times each in our prescribed lines. In Book II, fire functions, in part, as a metaphor for unbridled and destructive actions (see 'Snakes and fire' below). If the Greek warrior Pyrrhus embodies the horror of *furor*, then Aeneas and his men illustrate its folly and futility. When Aeneas first introduces himself in Book I, it is as *pius Aeneas* (378). Yet for the length of the poem this epithet remains a provisional one requiring determination and self-denial, at times, to prevent *pietas* lapsing into its opposite, *furor*, 'blind fury'.

When we first meet Aeneas in the poem, he is, in some important regards, the unfinished article. The poem begins with a state of turmoil. Aeneas has escaped Troy and is on the run after the Greek army, by the ploy of a huge wooden horse, has sacked his city. When we first meet our hero in the text, we don't know how or when he fled, we don't know where he will seek refuge or even if he will survive. With barely any build-up, we find him on the deck of his ship, amid a storm which will swiftly shipwreck him and his fleet of survivors. The poem delivers us *in medias res*, as a Roman might say, 'into the thick of it'. The story starts with chaos and confusion – the literal splintering of ships, and the structural disorder of a narrative which does not begin 'at the beginning'. The story should begin with Aeneas abandoning Troy as it fell to the Greeks. Then he would sail around the Mediterranean for seven years, searching for somewhere new to settle. Between Sicily and North Africa his fleet would be shipwrecked. Virgil rejects that chronological narrative, however, in favour of a non-linear sequence. First comes the storm (Book I), then in flashback comes the fall (Book II) and the search for a settlement (Book III). By delaying the famous fall of Troy to the second book, the poem keeps us listening. It also gives us more time to get a sense of Aeneas before he begins his eyewitness account.

Aeneas arrives on the poem's second word (*arma virumque*, 'arms and the man'), but it takes a further ninety lines before we hear his name and see his person. It is a big moment in the poem, and what Virgil chooses to emphasize is not his strength or stature, but his vulnerability. The storm comes and 'the limbs of Aeneas instantly slackened in the cold; he groaned' (*extemplo Aeneae solvuntur frigore membra; ingemit* 1.92–3). He is, on first impression, hardly the hero we were expecting. Further into Book I, Aeneas looks more convincing: he cheers up his shipwrecked men; hunts on their behalf; interacts with his mother, Venus; and plays the diplomat with Queen Dido of Carthage, where his ships wash up. But as we move into Book II, our initial impression still lingers of a hero who is, so far, sub-heroic. The early emphasis on his human frailty invites us to judge Aeneas more carefully, and on different terms, than if he were a two-dimensional fearless leader. We are intrigued by his past, and what experience he carries with him, as well as by his future and how he will fulfil those prophecies.

The delay of Troy's fall also allows the poem to do some key early exposition in Book I. We need a Homeric proem (I.1–11). The gods, and their rivalries, need introducing. Jupiter needs to pronounce what Fate has determined (I.254–96). We need to enter Carthage in North Africa, where Aeneas and his fleet find themselves (I.507–612). And we need to meet Dido, its queen, who will hold a feast and ask Aeneas to narrate how Troy fell (I.723–56). By the time we begin Book II and hushed silence falls (*conticuere omnes* 1), we're invested in much more than the dramatic collapse of Troy. Of course, we want to know why the Trojans took in the Wooden Horse. We want to hear how the Greeks ran amok and how King Priam met his end. But we are also curious as to how Aeneas, as a survivor, remembers the events and his part in them. We are a secondary audience listening in Dido's court, but we are no less invested than the Carthaginians in a story which we know must be one-sided, selective and emotional. The poem's focus expands beyond merely what happened at Troy. We are interested in the psychological strain on our protagonist both then, when the fighting raged, and now, when he can recollect with hindsight.

Narratorial standpoint

It is possible to relay much of the plot of Book II simply as a catalogue of Aeneas' failings:

- He is asleep when the Greeks enter.
- He instantly forgets the instructions of Hector.

- His counter-attack ends with every comrade dead.
- His defence of the palace roof is ineffectual.
- He fails to save Priam.
- His wife and father have to read the omens on his behalf.
- He loses Creusa as he leaves.

Virgil delivers us a hero who is either hesitant or overhasty. If this is a problem, it is not necessarily of the poet's own making. The sheer fact of Aeneas' survival, when every other Trojan hero falls, is problematic. Was he a coward? Did he collude with the enemy? Does he deserve the stature of his destiny? Virgil addresses this problem by appointing Aeneas as the narrator and thereby aligning him closely with his audiences – us and Dido. As we read Book II, we develop a sort of twofold awareness of what is happening within the narrative and what is happening within the narrator.

The book's content falls broadly into three parts:

> line 249: The Horse enters. [Sinon, Laocoon]
> line 558: Troy is overrun. [Hector, Priam]
> line 804: Aeneas escapes. [*Helen*, Venus, Anchises, Creusa]

See companion website for the disputed authenticity of the Helen episode (567–87).

Despite his status as the city's most prominent survivor, Aeneas does not locate himself in the city until line 271 (*mihi*). From here the narrative follows Aeneas around the city's streets, documenting Troy's destruction through his actions and interactions with certain notable characters (in brackets above). As we follow Aeneas' account at street level, we feel like we're in Troy, even though we're in Carthage. The audience is engaged in a more active response because we are constantly having to juxtapose the present (Carthage) and the past (Troy). This is a source of dramatic tension: we know at the beginning of Aeneas' narrative that it has a sad ending, but this also allows us to scrutinize Aeneas' perception of what happened. We have to keep asking how Aeneas participates in the events he reports. How directly will he describe his own failings? Will he show his heroic potential in how he evaluates what happened?

Narratorial self-awareness is rarely explicit in Book II, but when it does occur it jumps out, for example in *arma amens capio* (314n.). Most of the time we are left to infer how Aeneas feels as he revisits the sacking of Troy. Why, for instance, does he assign himself no part in the Sinon episode, other than the occasional first-person plural which puts him in the crowd (25, 105, 212, 234, 248)? Why do his narratorial reflections address the treachery of Greeks and the reversal of Trojan fortunes, but not his own failure to challenge Sinon or defend Laocoon?

Aeneas' instinct as hindsight narrator is to generalize rather than particularize; his reflections pull out the historical and ethical significance of critical moments. This distinguishes crucially the Aeneas who tells the story from the Aeneas who charges around the burning city. Aeneas' first reference to himself in the first-person singular is *mihi* 271, when he meets Hector's ghost. This scene is a point of transition for Aeneas, thematically but also narratorially. We see events through his eyes: the narrative focus is 'subjective' in that our perception of what's happening is channelled very strongly through Aeneas. The switch to a more subjective narrative for the poem's middle third differentiates the earlier, more 'collective' narrative of the Sinon episode. It also makes evident that Virgil's choice of Aeneas as hindsight narrator was not the only way to align his audience with his hero. The *Aeneid* could have begun with the fall of Troy told by a third-person narrator whose description of the event was filtered through Aeneas. The advantage of Aeneas narrating in Book II, as mentioned above, is that Virgil thereby commits his audience to a process of triangulation, responding always to both Aeneas the internal actor and Aeneas the external narrator.

There is another advantage too. Once the narrative becomes more subjective in its focus, Virgil is able to transfer that focus more freely to other subjects within the narrative. The name for this is *focalization*: temporarily giving the narrative from the standpoint of a certain individual. From the appearance of Hector's ghost, Virgil is able more naturally to shift the focal point within the narrative. There are some memorable examples of this in Book II: the description of Laocoon's spear (231n.); the flight of Panthus (318–21); Pyrrhus' assault on the palace doors (482–3); and the departure of Iulus (723–4). The Pyrrhus example illustrates the technique especially well. When Pyrrhus hacks a 'window' (*fenestram* 482) through the door of Priam's palace, the narrative is focalized through him because the splintered hole in the door is only a 'window' for him, the person looking through it. Aeneas is still narrating nominally, but from the palace rooftop he has minimal narratorial authority at this moment. The household only 'becomes visible' (*apparet* 483) and the interior chambers only 'reveal themselves' (*patescunt* 483) to Pyrrhus because, unlike Aeneas, he is looking eagerly into the palace for the first time.

Sinon and Laocoon

Sinon and Laocoon are two antagonists who never actually meet, but they are richly drawn in contradistinction. Together they establish and embody the tension between *dolus* ('trickery') and *virtus* ('integrity') which will shade much of the action in *Aeneid* II, culminating in the death of Priam – a king of proverbial *virtus* who is abandoned by the gods as he clutches their very altar (*quos ipse sacraverat ignes* 502).

Virgil's treatment of the Horse narrative takes its cue from Homer's *Odyssey*, where it features twice, recalled first by Menelaus during the feast of Book IV (266–89) and then sung by Demodocus to Odysseus in Book VIII (499–513). On neither occasion is there a hint of triumphalism. In fact, the prevailing mood among the Greek victors is sorrow: Odysseus even breaks down in tears (521–3). Here the *Odyssey*, as with the *Iliad*, invites us to problematize what it means to 'win' a war. This is a concern of the *Aeneid*, too, but in Book II the emphasis is as much on the problem of *how* a war is won, as on *what* is eventually won. This is one reason why Virgil departs from Homer and inserts the figure of Sinon into the Trojan assembly. In fact, in *Odyssey* VIII the Horse has been brought in prior to the Trojans' pivotal debate, in which neither Sinon nor Laocoon is involved. What, then, is the value to the *Aeneid* of these two figures?

Sinon is the epitome of Greek *dolus*: both his name and his narrative evoke our word 'sinuous', from the Latin *sinus*, 'coil'. When the snakes kill Laocoon, terror 'slithers into' the Trojans' hearts (*insinuat* 229), a metaphor equally apt for Sinon's rhetoric, which coils itself incrementally around its listeners.

As you read Sinon's three speeches (77–104; 108–44; 154–94) and analyse their design, you will notice many hallmarks of classic rhetoric: neat structure, explicit (if deceptive) logic, expressive syntax, emotional crescendoes, suggestive pauses, and more. A speech so precisely tooled, however, can also feel inauthentic, even alienating. The exemplary mid-Republican, Cato the Elder (234–149 BC), distinguished between Greek rhetorical polish and the rough-edged but authentic Roman style: 'the words of the Greeks are drawn from their lips; but Roman words come from the heart' (Plutarch, *Cato Maior* 12.5). Sinon's 'impromptu' speeches succeed despite their artifice because he calibrates his words so precisely to the psychological state of his audience, and in the first third of Book II we probably learn more about the Trojans, characterized implicitly, than we do about Sinon. The critic Maurice Bowra once described Book II as 'the poetry of defeat from the point of view of the defeated', and in the Sinon episode we see a citizen body too exhausted by war, too relieved, to notice their own naivety and optimism. When the Trojans respond to Sinon's script with tears and pity at 145, we imagine them crying also for their own enormous suffering (*laborum/tantorum* 143–4) and all the injustices they have endured (*animi non digna ferentes* 144).

Sinon exploits this collective feeling effectively, and his artful duplicity prevails over Laocoon's instinctive outburst. The contrast in their language mirrors the contrast in their moral status. Laocoon's speech characterizes him as an honest and vigorous man, albeit stubborn and brusque. His words fly out (*et procul* 42) as he runs down to avert danger. His rhetorical questions are blunt but incisive. In fact, his brevity and simplicity evoke the description of Cato's own speaking style (Cicero, *Brutus* 65–9). It is significant that Virgil chooses, at the start of the *Aeneid*, to kill off both Laocoon and what he represents, a more primitive but more responsible citizenship. We are urged to weigh the appeal of his integrity against its inefficacy, and to ask whether Laocoon is morally superior or just naïve.

Laocoon is one of several priest figures in Book II who are doomed to fall with the city, despite their priestly *virtus*. Both Coroebus and Priam will die poignantly at altars and another devout Trojan, Panthus, dies with the detail that neither his *pietas* nor his priesthood could protect him (*pietas nec Apollinis infula texit* 430). These deaths, and their sacrificial overtones (cf. Laocoon's bull simile), expose the tragic dissonance between human call and divine response. The brutal conclusion of the Trojan War takes no account of Laocoon's positive traits or those of Panthus, Coroebus and Priam.

Snakes and fire

Book II contains two dominant metaphors – snakes and fire – which offer a key to understanding the fall of Troy within the poem's thematic whole.

Already in the poem's first book, fire has been established as a symbol of disorder: Juno's actions inflame Venus (*urit atrox Iuno* I.662) and Cupid kindles a doomed love within Dido (*donisque furentem incendat reginam* I.659–60). In Book II, the dramatic setting of a burning city illuminated against the night sky allows Virgil to enlarge the fire metaphor, which is sustained up until a new day dawns in line 801 and Aeneas' tale ends. Fire imagery then returns at the end of the Dido narrative in Book IV, where *furor* is figured as fire from the book's opening (*caeco carpitur igni* 2) until the suicide of Dido (*accensa furore* 697).

In Book II, flames engulf the city literally (311n.) and metaphorically at various moments of chaos and destruction: the arrival of the snakes from Tenedos (210n.), the desperate skirmishing of Aeneas and his men (316n.), and the rampage of Pyrrhus (529n.). Forms of *ardeo* ('I burn') occur nine times in Book II, seven of those in the A Level prescription, and Virgil uses the slippage between its literal and its metaphorical meaning ('I yearn') to suggest the danger of impulsive behaviour, and in the case of Aeneas, the folly and futility of his fightback.

Pyrrhus, who rips through the royal palace like an indiscriminate fire, is slightly different. His imagery, even his name (469n.), connects the fire metaphor with *furor*, that sense of excessive, selfish anger and irrationality which he embodies and which Virgil warns against in the *Aeneid*. He is not the only character to use a form of *furo* or *furor* in Book II, and its wide application to other humans (244, 316, 345, 355), to gods (613) and to nature (304, 498), conveys the destructive potential within all of us and within nature.

If fire can destroy, it can also kindle and create, and towards the end of Book II this alternative status is suggested by the omen of a flame dancing on Iulus' head (683–4). This positive omen, attached to the child who will one day lead the Romans, invokes the religious and domestic value of fire. The fire symbol now has an ambivalent meaning. Virgil's language at this moment also links fire with the book's other main metaphor, snakes. The two verbs used for the flame on Iulus' head, *lambo* and *pascor*, mirror those used by the snakes from Tenedos who lick their lips (*lambebant* 211) and devour their prey (*depascitur* 215). The verbal echo connects snakes with fire and hints that both metaphors can have a positive as well as a negative construction. They can represent both productive and destructive transformation.

Nature is the predominant source of similes in Virgil, as in Homer and two other epic antecedents which these similes respond to, Apollonius' *Argonautica* (third century BC) and Lucretius' *De Rerum Natura* (first century BC). Two of Book II's nine similes involve a snake: Androgeos retreats as if from a snake (379–81) and Pyrrhus appears like a snake after hibernation (471–5). Alongside these explicit references there are persistent allusions to snakes and snake-like behaviour which establish their importance as a metaphor in Book II. Snakes are associated early on with insidious behaviour: Sinon's name, discussed above, suggests insidious coiling, and the first snake simile characterizes Trojans who are about to ambush (Latin *insidiae*) unwitting Greeks. The Horse, an insidious contraption, slithers into Troy (*lapsus* 236) just as the snakes from Tenedos slither up to the temple of Athena (*lapsu* 225). The Horse is pregnant with weapons (238 *feta armis*) just as Pyrrhus' snake is swollen (*tumidum* 472) after gorging on toxic grass (*mala gramina pastus* 471).

Snakes can menace and kill, like Pyrrhus, but snakes also slough their skin and regenerate, hence their association with the healing god Asclepius. In line 471, *pastus* derives from *pascor*, the verb used both for the snakes of Tenedos and the flame of Iulus. By transferring a part of *pascor* from the snakes to fire, Virgil confirms a positive association between these two images in the way that recurring parts of *ardens* had conveyed their dangerous dimension (529n.). Soon after the flame of Iulus, the second omen of a falling star glides over the rooftops of Troy using the other major snake verb, *labor* (*labentem* 695). The recurrence of these words in the book's last quarter restores to snakes and fire their positive potential, and the ambivalence of these two metaphors conveys the tension throughout the poem between the productive and destructive tendencies innate within humans and the world.

Intertextuality

Our earliest surviving portrait of Virgil, a mosaic from Tunisia, shows the poet seated between Clio and Melopomene, the muses of History and Tragedy. The image speaks to Virgil's subject matter and his sensibilities; it also speaks to his vigorous engagement with a range of literary antecedents. As well as historiography (see pp.6–7), the *Aeneid* engages heavily with its epic forebears, especially Homer, and with the tragic drama of fifth-century Greece.

Homer's epics are the principal intertexts, and the *Aeneid*'s first half is often called 'Odyssean', for its sea voyage, and the second half 'Iliadic', for its pitched battles. Such a division is attractive but simplistic: *Aeneid* II, for instance, is far more Iliadic than Odyssean. Virgil's engagement with Homer is more complex than first appearances suggest. As T. S. Eliot once said, an immature poet imitates and a mature poet steals. Take one early example: the introduction of Aeneas in Book I. Like Homer (*Od.* 5.278f.), Virgil uses a storm to put his protagonist to the test, introducing him in a do-or-die predicament, facing hostile conditions and an indignant god. Unlike Odysseus, though, Aeneas is surrounded by his men. His task is not purely to preserve himself; he must also keep a cool head and look out for others. Virgil's engagement with Homer is revealed by showing, not telling, that Aeneas must be a different kind of hero to Odysseus. Virgil's intertextuality is a dynamic of adopting, adapting, converging and diverging, in order to create additional meaning.

Book II also engages with the conventions of a Greek tragic messenger speech. For much of the book it is easy to forget that Aeneas is our narrator because he reports so much direct speech in the Sinon episode, and his omniscient narrative at the palace of Priam often feels impersonal. Yet when, for example, Aeneas emphasizes his eyewitness authority (*vidi ipse* 499; *vidi* 501), it is more fruitful to view him as a Greek tragic messenger, making the conventional claim of 'narratorial autopsy', than as mistaken or dishonest because he was actually on the rooftop when Priam died. In this light, too, we might view the frequency of *ecce* in Book II (402n.). The 'epitaphs' for Troy (241f.) and Priam (554f.) likewise belong to a Greek tragic messenger. It could be that Virgil is using Aeneas' narrator status to respond to Troy tragedies that have not survived: we know, for instance, that Euripides wrote a tragedy called *Sinon*; Sophocles wrote a *Laocoon*; and all three Athenian tragedians wrote a *Palamedes*. It could also be that Virgil designates Aeneas as a tragic messenger in order to amplify the tragic irony which suffuses much of *Aeneid* II, especially the Sinon episode (44n., 160n.).

Interrogating intertexts is worthwhile simply because more meaning becomes available. For a school-level student, though, the operation of allusion and intertext can quickly distract from the core business of engaging with what is there in the text and turning those words into meaning. In the case of *Aeneid* II, your intertextual attention is required predominantly for the similes: there are more of these (nine) than in any other book of the *Aeneid* and they all have at least one Homeric antecedent.

Similes

Below is a list of the similes found in *Aeneid* II. All but 3 and 9 are found in the prescribed A level lines.

1. Laocoon roars like a wounded bull (223–4)
2. Aeneas on his roof listens like a shepherd (304–8)
3. Aeneas and his comrades rush on like wolves (355–8)
4. Androgeos retreats as if from a snake (379–81)
5. Battle lines clash like warring winds (416–19)
6. Pyrrhus emerges like a snake from hibernation (471–5)
7. Greeks burst into the palace like a rampant river (496–9)
8. Hecuba and her daughters cower like doves in a storm (516)
9. Troy crashes to its ruin like a felled tree (626–31)

Similes vary in length, as you can see, and also significance. The basic function of a simile is to illustrate A by comparison to B:

<u>Laocoon bellowed</u> (A)   **like** a wounded bull fleeing the altar. (B)

It is left for the reader to infer what the point of the comparison is – i.e., what about B is equivalent to A? The primary point of comparison is usually obvious: Laocoon bellows like a wounded bull because he is also hurt and frightened. But the characteristics of A and B can overlap to a greater or lesser degree: Laocoon can roar in pain, of course, but not exactly as a bull would. Where A and B do and don't overlap is often significant. In the case of Laocoon's simile, he is preparing to *make* a sacrifice when the snakes attack, unlike the imaginary bull which is preparing to *be* a sacrifice. The simile actually contains a dissimilarity as well as a similarity, and there is meaning in that discrepancy: Laocoon is devout but to no avail (cf. Priam), and his death can be viewed as some sort of sacrifice which facilitates the sad fate of the Trojans. Broader still, it might evoke the fictitious sacrifice of Sinon (122–36), or the sacrifice of Iphigenia (116–17) at the beginning of the Trojan War, or the poem's wider concern with the human cost of empire (see pp.7–10, 'The status of Aeneas').

The simile is a descriptive technique, but in a narrative epic we can expect it to interact richly with the surrounding narrative. A mid-narrative simile allows the reader to dwell on not just what the simile signifies but also what has happened in the action prior and what might happen next. This is a source of tension – the action is suspended until the simile is over – but more importantly it invites the audience to integrate the descriptive detail into the wider narrative, or characterization, or themes. Such 'correspondences' will sometimes be encouraged by a verbal or visual cue. In Aeneas' shepherd simile, for example, the trees are hauled headlong (*praecipites* 307) by the floodwater. Ten lines later, the impulsive anger of Aeneas hauls headlong (*praecipitat* 317) his rationality. The verbal echo connects what Aeneas has seen with his emotional reaction; it also suggests that his *furor* is no less natural – and no more desirable – than a flash flood.

Lastly, there may be degrees of correspondence between Virgil's simile and an antecedent. Familiarity with these is probably beyond the scope of A Level, but for interest's sake you will find some of the antecedents cited in the commentary notes.

On the companion website is a worked analysis of Pyrrhus' snake simile (471–5) which illustrates how to extract meaning from one of Virgil's similes.

Sound

Classical poetry was written to be read aloud, and Virgil himself was credited with an expressive reading voice (*Vita* 29). A poet could write into their poem a range of sound effects in order to suggest or support meanings in their text, just as a film score interacts with the visual content and speech of a scene. Some of these sound effects will be familiar from English poetry: alliteration, assonance and onomatopoeia are good examples. English poets, unlike Virgil, can also call on punctuation to stress certain words, or alter their pitch, or to indicate pauses as their poem is read aloud. Virgil's poetry can, however, call on its metre – the dactylic hexameter – to catch the ear and create correspondences between the sound of a line and its content.

A poem's metre is its system of patterning syllables within each line. Virgil's choice of dactylic hexameter followed the precedent for epic poetry set by Ennius, who was himself adopting the metre of Homer. Classical metres arranged syllables by their length (long or short) rather than their stress accent, as English does. Natural stress accent did exist in the Roman world – 'head' is *cap*ut not cap*ut* – but it was a secondary characteristic as far as metre was concerned.

A line of dactylic hexameter contains six *metra* or metrical 'feet', and each foot comprises two or three syllables. The first four can be either a dactyl (DUM-dee-dee) or a spondee (DUM-dum). The fifth foot is almost always a dactyl, but very rarely a spondee (*circumspexit* 68). The sixth foot can be either a trochee (DUM-dee) or a spondee. We identify and mark syllable length using – for long syllables and ∪ for short, in a process called 'scansion'.

dactyl   – ∪ ∪
spondee   – –
trochee   – ∪

This is how a line of dactylic hexameter looks in full, with each foot marked off by a vertical line.

```
 – –      |– –      |– –      |– –      |– –      |– –
 – ∪ ∪   |– ∪ ∪   |– ∪ ∪   |– ∪ ∪   |– ∪ ∪   |– ∪
```

When you 'scan' the sixth foot, it is conventional to put an 'x' for the last syllable because its length can vary according to how a reader rolls onto the next line. The 'x' is called an *anceps* (lit. 'doubtful thing').

A line of hexameter will range from twelve to seventeen syllables in length, and that range gives a poet room for artistic variation. Compare this to how a drummer might vary a groove, or add in fills, while maintaining a backbeat within a single time signature.

For first-time scanners, the biggest challenge is usually working out whether each syllable in the line is long or short. A syllable can be long either by nature or by position.

Naturally long syllables are those containing a long vowel (e.g., *dē-super*) or a diphthong (*ae, au, oe, ei*). Syllables at the end of words are usually familiar inflections which you are used to hearing often; this makes the deduction easier. We know that the ablative plural of first and second declensions is long (*-īs*), for example, whereas the third declension genitive ending is short (*-ĭs*), and so on. The length of stem syllables, however, may be less obvious – even with GCSE words. An altar, for example, is *āra* not *ăra*. In the case of new or indeclinable words, like *ilicet* (424), it's even tougher (*īlĭcĕt*). Dictionaries will usually mark those stem vowels which are naturally long.

Positionally long syllables are short vowels which become long when followed by two or more consonants – either in their word (e.g., *ōmnis*) or in their line (e.g., *aliquīs latet* 48). There is an exception to this rule: when the second consonant is *l* or *r*, the syllable can be either long or short (see *prima* below). Also note:

- A vowel before another vowel is short, unless they form a diphthong (e.g., *fŭisset*);
- *qu-* is treated as a single consonant (e.g., *equus* = two syllables);
- *x* (*cs*) and *z* (*sd*) are treated as double consonants;
- An initial *i-* followed by a vowel is consonantal, equivalent to modern *j* (e.g., *iacio* = three syllables). The *-i-* in *huius* and *cuius* is consonantal.

Elision is the process whereby a terminal vowel (e.g., *ib-i*) blends with an initial vowel (e.g., *ibi a-nte*). This is frequent enough in Virgil that it is worth starting your line scansion by identifying any elisions. Bracket off the terminal vowel and discount it as you scan the rest of the line (e.g., *ib(i) ante*). Also note:

- *-am*, *-um*, *-em*, *-im* or *-om* at the end of a word elides as if the *-m* were absent (e.g., *incens(am) et* 555);
- An initial *h-* should be ignored when scanning.

Caesura (from (*Musa*) **caesura**, 'the Muse about to cut') is the name given to a word-break within a metrical foot, usually after the first syllable – the syllable which has additional emphasis as the 'first beat of the bar' (technical term, *ictus*). A hexameter usually has a principal caesura, a more prominent pause, after the first syllable of the third foot, around halfway in the line. If there is no strong third-foot caesura, one will land in the fourth foot, often accompanied by one in the second foot too. We mark caesurae using a double vertical line.

Below you will find scanned three lines of the prescribed text (97–9) which demonstrate most of the rules above.

$$- \quad \cup\cup| - \cup \; \cup|-||-|- \quad -| - \cup \; \cup|-\cup$$
97   hinc mihi p͟rima mali   labes, (h)inc semper Ulixes

$$- \cup\cup|-||-|-\cup \; \cup|- || \; - \; |- \cup\cup|--$$
98   criminibus terrere novis, (h)inc spargere voces

$$- - | \quad - \cup \cup|-||- | -\cup\cup|- \; \cup\cup| - \cup$$
99   in vulg(um) ambiguas   et quaerere conscius arma

The skill of scansion is important for two reasons. Firstly, it can help you disambiguate endings which appear identical on the page. In line 97, above, the short *-a* of *primă* allows us to rule out the feminine ablative singular (*primā*) as a possible parsing, for example. Secondly, a basic awareness of Virgil's metrical dexterity will boost your literary appreciation and at A Level, knowledgable and relevant reference to metre is credit-worthy in the 15-mark commentary question. The companion website contains additional information on the interplay of *ictus* and stress accent, as well as further reading and a worked analysis of how Virgil uses his metre expressively in lines 314–17.

Practical criticism: where to begin?

Practical criticism is a two-part exercise: first, construe meaning(s) in a given passage; second, articulate how details of language, structure and form express that meaning. Below, you will find a structured approach to interrogating any given passage. It is not exhaustive, nor definitive, but there is more than enough to give you that first foothold. The companion website contains an example of worked analysis, written with the OCR A Level criteria in mind.

i. What is happening?

- What is happening in the passage?
- What happens before and after this passage?
- Is the passage narrative, description or direct speech – or a blend?
- Who is narrating/describing/speaking?
- How would you characterize their tone?
- Is there more than one audience?
- What is the status of each character?
- What is the relationship between characters?
- Is there a prevailing mood or atmosphere?
- How does this passage develop a character or theme or tension?

ii. How is it organized?

a) Macro-level

- How does the passage progress?
- How many sentences are there?

- What type: statement, question, command, exclamation?
- What is the degree of detail?
- What allusions, if any, are active?

b) Micro-level

- Which actions get main verb status?
- How simple or complex is the syntax?
- How does this affect the pace of the passage?
- Are details or ideas enlarged by successive phrases?
- Is there symmetry or juxtaposition in the arrangement of phrases or clauses?
- How compressed is the sense of a phrase or clause?
- Is there any meaningful ambiguity?
- How do details move us closer or further from the narrative?
- What types of detail are there (e.g., domestic, military, emotional)?
- How do connectives signpost the passage (e.g., **ecce 57** or **at 486**)?
- What is included and excluded from the narrative focus?
- Is the narrative focus aligned with a particular character?

iii. Word order

- How does the word order deviate from 'default prose' word order?
- What word is prominent at the head or tail of the line?
- Is the line end-stopped or enjambed?
- Why does the enjambment break where it does?
- Where are adverbs and adjectives situated relative to their verb or noun?
- Are key words promoted or deferred within their phrase or clause?

- Is there repetitive patterning: alliteration, anaphora, chiasmus, epanalepsis, polyptoton, tricolon?
- Does the word order reflect or enact the content somehow?

iv. Why that word?

a) Lexical

- How close is this word to its commonest usage?
- What are the connotations of this word, in the *Aeneid* and elsewhere?
- Is this word being used literally or metaphorically, or both?
- What is the register of this word (e.g., Homeric, tragic, colloquial, legal, etc.)?
- Are any words near-impossible to translate in English?

b) Grammatical

- Is the passage unusually dense in verb forms, or nouns or descriptors?
- Why this particular verb form (e.g., participle)? Is the voice/mood/tense/person of this verb a literary choice?
- Does the flow of verb tenses change emphatically?
- Are personal pronouns deployed emphatically?

v. What images are generated?

- What sorts of metaphor are there (e.g., simile, personification)?
- How do these characterize the thing/person being figured?
- Is the description more concrete or abstract?
- How hard does your mind's eye have to work?
- Does metaphorical language build cumulatively within the passage?
- Does the image resonate with a passage elsewhere?

vi. How does it sound?

- Is there alliteration/consonance/assonance in the clustering of words?
- How does the repetition of words or phrases catch the ear?
- What is the split of dactyls to spondees in the first four feet?
- How do the dactyls/spondees affect the pace or the tone of the line?
- What words land before or after the principal caesura?
- How does elision emphasize the relationship between words?
- How coordinated is the ictus and accent, especially in the final two feet?

Literary terms

Below is some critical vocabulary which may help you clarify your analysis. Note that many of these terms are essentially variants of four basic technique-types: repetition, metaphor, antithesis and emphatic word order.

These terms are asterisked when they occur in the Commentary Notes.

alliteration The clustering of words which start with the same letter. **44 dona carere dolis Danaum**. See also 84, 107, 192, 209, 418. A sub-species of consonance (see below).

anacoluthon When a syntactical unit breaks off mid-flow, or morphs into a new construction. **522 non, si ipse meus nunc adforet Hector.**

anaphora Repetition at the start of successive lines, phrases or clauses. **54 si fata deum, si mens non laeva fuisset**. See also 137–8, 143–4, 157–8, 283–4, 483–4, 554.

aposiopesis When a speaker dramatically or emotionally clams up, leaving their speech incomplete. **100 nec requievit enim, donec Calchante ministro --.**

apostrophe When a speaker 'turns away' to suddenly address in the second-person someone or something not actually present. **56 Priamique arx alta maneres.**

archaism A word or idiom borrowed from an earlier period of Latin. **524 sic ore effata.** See also 48, 75, 100, 467.

assonance The clustering of vowel sounds within words or within lines. **165 fatale adgressi sacrato avellere.** See also 47, 190, 223, 494.

asyndeton The omission of conjunctions. **294 hos cape fatorum comites, his moenia quaere.** See also 306, 438–9.

chiasmus The ABBA patterning of words, by grammatical agreement, part of speech, alliteration, etc. **494 rumpunt aditus primosque trucidant.** See also 281, 416, 483.

consonance The clustering of consonants or consonant-groups within words (also known as 'internal alliteration') or within lines. **206 pectora quorum inter fluctus arrecta.** See also 433, 494.

enjambment When the sense runs over the end of a line. **212–13 illi agmine certo / Laocoonta petunt.** See also 400, 448, 505.

epanalepsis When a word in a phrase or clause recurs, with no grammatical impact, at the end of that phrase or clause. **405–6 ad caelum tendens ardentia lumina frustra / lumina.**

hendiadys When a noun and adjective pair is instead expressed as two nouns. **534 voci iraeque** (=*voci iratae*). See also 92, 470.

hypallage When an adjective which naturally qualifies one thing is transferred instead to a neighbouring noun. **231 sceleratam intorserit hastam** (=*sceleratus intorserit hastam*). See also 51, 135.

hyperbaton An emphatic deviation from typical word order, usually meaning distance between an adjective and its noun. **228–9 novus per pectora cunctis / insinuat pavor.** See also 113, 374, 446.

hysteron proteron When a sequence of actions in the narrative inverts the natural chronological order. **47 inspectura domos venturaque desuper urbi**.

juxtaposition When words are positioned immediately next to one another in order to convey some relationship between them; e.g., mutual reinforcement, or antithesis. **48 error equo**. See also 101, 269, 276, 310, 529.

litotes Emphasis by understatement, often using a double negative formula. **91 haud ignota**. See also 154.

metaphor Figuring something as something it is not. Variants of this are the simile, introduced by 'as' or 'like', and personification, which specifically figures something as human. **97 prima mali labes** (metaphor); **306 sata laeta** (personification). See also 155, 397, 504.

metonymy When something is denoted solely by an attribute or an association. **99 arma**, meaning 'battles'. See also 311, 440.

mimesis At line-level, this refers to the imitation of content or meaning in linguistic or metrical detail; e.g., by word order (**482 ingentem . . . fenestram**) or by elision (**99 vulgum ambiguas**).

onomatopoeia When a word's sound corroborates its meaning. **135 limosoque lacu**. See also 209.

parataxis When ideas are sequenced adjacent to one another in short, simple sentences which resist the tendency of Latin to combine and connect by subordination. **290–1 hostis habet muros; ruit alto a culmine Troia. sat patriae Priamoque datum**. See also 172, 442–4.

pleonasm The emphatic over-expression of a detail. **40 primus ibi ante omnes**. See also 50.

polyptoton The repetition of a word in changed form, morphological or cognate. **80 finxit . . . finget**. See also 53, 154, 160, 498–9.

synecdoche When a part of something is used to denote its whole. **186 roboribus textis**, meaning the entire Horse. See also 209.

tragic irony A form of dramatic irony where the narrator and audience know that events in the narrative will end unhappily, but the characters do not. Their obliviousness can give a tragic flavour to narrative details as well as their own words and actions. **44 sic notus Ulixes.** See also 237, 385, 488, 536.

tricolon A sequence of three sense-units (words, phrases, clauses), often ascending in length or intensity. **451–2 regis succurrere tectis / auxilioque levare viros vimque addere victis.**

zeugma When a single verb governs two nouns but the verb's usage differs in each case, for example having both a literal and non-literal application. **378 pedem cum voce repressit.**

Further reading

Two excellent, modern introductions to the *Aeneid* are Alison Keith's *Virgil* (Bloomsbury, 2020), Ch.4, 'Aeneis'; and William Fitzgerald's *How to Read a Latin Poem* (OUP, 2013), Ch.4, 'Vergil: The Unclassical Classic'.

William Anderson's *The Art of the Aeneid* (BCP, 1989), has a valuable chapter (Ch.2) on the poem's first two books, and R. D. Williams' *Aeneas and the Roman Hero*, (BCP, 1998), explores what makes Aeneas heroic in Ch.3, 'Aeneas: The New Hero'.

In terms of journal articles, there are three must-reads:

- K. W. Gransden, 'The Fall of Troy', *Greece and Rome* 32.1 (1985): 60–72.
- Bernard M. Knox, 'The Serpent and the Flame: The Imagery of the Second Book of the Aeneid', *American Journal of Philology* 71.4 (1950): 379–400.
- John P. Lynch, 'Laocoön and Sinon: Virgil Aeneid 2.40—198', *Greece and Rome* 27.2 (1980): 170–9.

And one bonus:

- A. M. Bowie, 'The Death of Priam: Allegory and History in the Aeneid', *Classical Quarterly* 40.2 (1990): 470–81.

Each of these articles is available through JSTOR.

Aeneid II has been well served by commentators over the last 150 years. The most recent, and comprehensive, is Nicholas Horsfall's (Brill, 2008): imperious, but expensive. More readily available is R. G. Austin's edition (OUP, 1964), a text which gives full due to Virgil as a poet and the *Aeneid* as a poem. The school-level commentary of H. E. Gould and J. L. Whiteley (BCP, 1982), is also easy to access.

Additional works cited in this volume:

- C. M. Bowra, *From Virgil to Milton*, Macmillan, 1945.
- Gordon Willis Williams, *Technique and Ideas in the* Aeneid, Yale UP, 1983.

The text following uses the edition of Virgil's works produced by Sir Roger Mynors in 1969 as part of the Oxford Classical Texts series.

Text

1–39: Aeneas is asked by his host, Queen Dido of Carthage, to relay how Troy fell to the Greek army. He begins with the building of the Wooden Horse and the duplicitous departure of the Greeks. His fellow Trojans find the horse and puzzle over its purpose.

primus ibi ante omnes, magna comitante caterva,   40
Laocoon ardens summa decurrit ab arce,
et procul: 'o miseri, quae tanta insania, cives?
creditis avectos hostes? aut ulla putatis
dona carere dolis Danaum? sic notus Ulixes?
aut hoc inclusi ligno occultantur Achivi,   45
aut haec in nostros fabricata est machina muros,
inspectura domos venturaque desuper urbi,
aut aliquis latet error: equo ne credite, Teucri.
quidquid id est, timeo Danaos et dona ferentes.'
sic fatus validis ingentem viribus hastam   50
in latus inque feri curvam compagibus alvum
contorsit. stetit illa tremens, uteroque recusso
insonuere cavae gemitumque dedere cavernae.
et, si fata deum, si mens non laeva fuisset,
impulerat ferro Argolicas foedare latebras   55
Troiaque nunc staret, Priamique arx alta maneres.
ecce, manus iuvenem interea post terga revinctum
pastores magno ad regem clamore trahebant
Dardanidae, qui se ignotum venientibus ultro,
hoc ipsum ut strueret Troiamque aperiret Achivis,   60
obtulerat, fidens animi atque in utrumque paratus,
seu versare dolos seu certae occumbere morti.
undique visendi studio Troiana iuventus
circumfusa ruit certantque inludere capto.

accipe nunc Danaum insidias et crimine ab uno 65
disce omnes.
namque ut conspectu in medio turbatus, inermis
constitit atque oculis Phrygia agmina circumspexit,
'heu, quae nunc tellus,' inquit, 'quae me aequora possunt
accipere? aut quid iam misero mihi denique restat, 70
cui neque apud Danaos usquam locus, et super ipsi
Dardanidae infensi poenas cum sanguine poscunt?'
quo gemitu conversi animi compressus et omnis
impetus. hortamur fari quo sanguine cretus,
quid-ve ferat; memoret quae sit fiducia capto. 75
[ille haec deposita tandem formidine fatur:]
'cuncta equidem tibi, rex, fuerit quodcumque, fatebor
vera', inquit; 'neque me Argolica de gente negabo.
hoc primum. nec, si miserum Fortuna Sinonem
finxit, vanum etiam mendacemque improba finget. 80
fando aliquod si forte tuas pervenit ad aures
Belidae nomen Palamedis et incluta fama
gloria, quem falsa sub proditione Pelasgi
insontem infando indicio, quia bella vetabat,
demisere neci, nunc cassum lumine lugent 85
illi me comitem et consanguinitate propinquum
pauper in arma pater primis huc misit ab annis.
dum stabat regno incolumis regumque vigebat
conciliis, et nos aliquod nomenque decusque
gessimus. invidia postquam pellacis Ulixi 90
(haud ignota loquor) superis concessit ab oris,
adflictus vitam in tenebris luctuque trahebam
et casum insontis mecum indignabar amici.
nec tacui demens et me, fors si qua tulisset,
si patrios umquam remeassem victor ad Argos, 95
promisi ultorem et verbis odia aspera movi.
hinc mihi prima mali labes, hinc semper Ulixes
criminibus terrere novis, hinc spargere voces

in vulgum ambiguas et quaerere conscius arma.
nec requievit enim, donec Calchante ministro -- 100
sed quid ego haec autem nequiquam ingrata revolvo,
quidve moror? si omnes uno ordine habetis Achivos,
idque audire sat est, iamdudum sumite poenas:
hoc Ithacus velit et magno mercentur Atridae.'
tum vero ardemus scitari et quaerere causas, 105
ignari scelerum tantorum artisque Pelasgae.
prosequitur pavitans et ficto pectore fatur:
'saepe fugam Danai Troia cupiere relicta
moliri et longo fessi discedere bello;
fecissentque utinam! saepe illos aspera ponti 110
interclusit hiems et terruit Auster euntes.
praecipue cum iam hic trabibus contextus acernis
staret equus, toto sonuerunt aethere nimbi.
suspensi Eurypylum scitatum oracula Phoebi
mittimus, isque adytis haec tristia dicta reportat: 115
'sanguine placastis ventos et virgine caesa,
cum primum Iliacas, Danai, venistis ad oras;
sanguine quaerendi reditus animaque litandum
Argolica.'' vulgi quae vox ut venit ad auris,
obstipuere animi gelidusque per ima cucurrit 120
ossa tremor, cui fata parent, quem poscat Apollo.

hic Ithacus vatem magno Calchanta tumultu
protrahit in medios; quae sint ea numina divum
flagitat. et mihi iam multi crudele canebant
artificis scelus, et taciti ventura videbant. 125
bis quinos silet ille dies tectusque recusat
prodere voce sua quemquam aut opponere morti.
vix tandem, magnis Ithaci clamoribus actus,
composito rumpit vocem et me destinat arae.
adsensere omnes et, quae sibi quisque timebat, 130
unius in miseri exitium conversa tulere.

A S

iamque dies infanda aderat; mihi sacra parari
et salsae fruges et circum tempora vittae.
eripui, fateor, leto me et vincula rupi,
limosoque lacu per noctem obscurus in ulva   135
delitui dum vela darent, si forte dedissent.
nec mihi iam patriam antiquam spes ulla videndi
nec dulces natos exoptatumque parentem,
quos illi fors et poenas ob nostra reposcent
effugia, et culpam hanc miserorum morte piabunt.   140
quod te per superos et conscia numina veri,
per si qua est quae restet adhuc mortalibus usquam
intemerata fides, oro, miserere laborum
tantorum, miserere animi non digna ferentis.'
his lacrimis vitam damus et miserescimus ultro.   145
ipse viro primus manicas atque arta levari
vincla iubet Priamus dictisque ita fatur amicis:
'quisquis es, amissos hinc iam obliviscere Graios
(noster eris) mihique haec edissere vera roganti:
quo molem hanc immanis equi statuere? quis auctor?   150
quidve petunt? quae religio? aut quae machina belli?'
dixerat. ille dolis instructus et arte Pelasga
sustulit exutas vinclis ad sidera palmas:
'vos, aeterni ignes, et non violabile vestrum
testor numen,' ait, 'vos arae ensesque nefandi,   155
quos fugi, vittaeque deum, quas hostia gessi:
fas mihi Graiorum sacrata resolvere iura,
fas odisse viros atque omnia ferre sub auras.
si qua tegunt, teneor patriae nec legibus ullis.
tu modo promissis maneas servataque serves   160
Troia fidem, si vera feram, si magna rependam.
omnis spes Danaum et coepti fiducia belli
Palladis auxiliis semper stetit. impius ex quo
Tydides sed enim scelerumque inventor Ulixes,
fatale adgressi sacrato avellere templo   165

Palladium caesis summae custodibus arcis,
corripuere sacram effigiem manibusque cruentis
virgineas ausi divae contingere vittas,
ex illo fluere ac retro sublapsa referri
spes Danaum, fractae vires, aversa deae mens.   170
nec dubiis ea signa dedit Tritonia monstris.
vix positum castris simulacrum: arsere coruscae
luminibus flammae arrectis, salsusque per artus
sudor iit, terque ipsa solo (mirabile dictu)
emicuit parmamque ferens hastamque trementem.   175
extemplo temptanda fuga canit aequora Calchas,
nec posse Argolicis exscindi Pergama telis
omina ni repetant Argis numenque reducant
quod pelágo et curvis secum avexere carinis.
et nunc quod patrias vento petiere Mycenas,   180
arma deosque parant comites pelagoque remenso
improvisi aderunt; ita digerit omina Calchas.
hanc pro Palladio moniti, pro numine laeso
effigiem statuere, nefas quae triste piaret.
hanc tamen immensam Calchas attollere molem   185
roboribus textis caeloque educere iussit,
ne recipi portis aut duci in moenia posset, ·
neu populum antiqua sub religione tueri.
nam si vestra manus violasset dona Minervae,
tum magnum exitium (quod di prius omen in ipsum   190
convertant!) Priami imperio Phrygibusque futurum;
sin manibus vestris vestram ascendisset in urbem,
ultro Asiam magno Pelopea ad moenia bello
venturam, et nostros ea fata manere nepotes.'
talibus insidiis periurique arte Sinonis   195
credita res, captique dolis lacrimisque coactis
quos neque Tydides nec Larisaeus Achilles,
non anni domuere decem, non mille carinae.
hic aliud maius miseris multoque tremendum

obicitur magis atque improvida pectora turbat.   200
Laocoon, ductus Neptuno sorte sacerdos,
sollemnes taurum ingentem mactabat ad aras.
ecce autem gemini a Tenedo tranquilla per alta
(horresco referens) immensis orbibus angues
incumbunt pelago pariterque ad litora tendunt;   205
pectora quorum inter fluctus arrecta iubaeque
sanguineae superant undas, pars cetera pontum
pone legit sinuatque immensa volumine terga.
fit sonitus spumante salo; iamque arva tenebant
ardentesque oculos suffecti sanguine et igni   210
sibila lambebant linguis vibrantibus ora.
diffugimus visu exsangues. illi agmine certo
Laocoonta petunt; et primum parva duorum
corpora natorum serpens amplexus uterque
implicat et miseros morsu depascitur artus;   215
post ipsum auxilio subeuntem ac tela ferentem
corripiunt spirisque ligant ingentibus; et iam
bis medium amplexi, bis collo squamea circum
terga dati superant capite et cervicibus altis.
ille simul manibus tendit divellere nodos   220
perfusus sanie vittas atroque veneno,
clamores simul horrendos ad sidera tollit:
quales mugitus, fugit cum saucius aram
taurus et incertam excussit cervice securim.
at gemini lapsu delubra ad summa dracones   225
effugiunt saevaeque petunt Tritonidis arcem,
sub pedibusque deae clipeique sub orbe teguntur.
tum vero tremefacta novus per pectora cunctis
insinuat pavor, et scelus expendisse merentem
Laocoonta ferunt, sacrum qui cuspide robur   230
laeserit et tergo sceleratam intorserit hastam.
ducendum ad sedes simulacrum orandaque divae
numina conclamant.

AS

dividimus muros et moenia pandimus urbis.
accingunt omnes operi pedibusque rotarum 235
subiciunt lapsus, et stuppea vincula collo
intendunt; scandit fatalis machina muros
feta armis. pueri circum innuptaeque puellae
sacra canunt funemque manu contingere gaudent;
illa subit mediaeque minans inlabitur urbi. 240
o patria, o divum domus Ilium et incluta bello
moenia Dardanidum! quater ipso in limine portae
substitit atque utero sonitum quater arma dedere;
instamus tamen immemores caecique furore
et monstrum infelix sacrata sistimus arce. 245
tunc etiam fatis aperit Cassandra futuris
ora dei iussu non umquam credita Teucris.
nos delubra deum miseri, quibus ultimus esset
ille dies, festa velamus fronde per urbem.

AS

250–67: As soon as night falls, the Greek fleet sails back from its location off the island of Tenedos. Sinon lets his concealed countrymen out of the Horse and they slaughter the guards at the city gates. The remainder of the Greek army floods into Troy.

tempus erat quo prima quies mortalibus aegris
incipit et dono divum gratissima serpit.
in somnis, ecce, ante oculos maestissimus Hector   270
visus adesse mihi largosque effundere fletus,
raptatus bigis, ut quondam, aterque cruento
pulvere perque pedes traiectus lora tumentes.
ei mihi, qualis erat, quantum mutatus ab illo
Hectore qui redit exuvias indutus Achilli   275
vel Danaum Phrygios iaculatus puppibus ignes!
squalentem barbam et concretos sanguine crines
vulneraque illa gerens, quae circum plurima muros
accepit patrios. ultro flens ipse videbar
compellare virum et maestas expromere voces: 280
'o lux Dardaniae, spes o fidissima Teucrum,
quae tantae tenuere morae? quibus Hector ab oris
expectate venis? ut te post multa tuorum
funera, post varios hominumque urbisque labores
defessi aspicimus! quae causa indigna serenos   285
foedavit vultus? aut cur haec vulnera cerno?'
ille nihil, nec me quaerentem vana moratur,
sed graviter gemitus imo de pectore ducens,
'heu fuge, nate dea, teque his' ait 'eripe flammis.
hostis habet muros; ruit alto a culmine Troia.   290
sat patriae Priamoque datum: si Pergama dextra
defendi possent, etiam hac defensa fuissent.
sacra suosque tibi commendat Troia penates;
hos cape fatorum comites, his moenia quaere
magna pererrato statues quae denique ponto.'   295
sic ait et manibus vittas Vestamque potentem

A
Level

aeternumque adytis effert penetralibus ignem.
diverso interea miscentur moenia luctu,
et magis atque magis, quamquam secreta parentis
Anchisae domus arboribusque obtecta recessit,   300
clarescunt sonitus armorumque ingruit horror.
excutior somno et summi fastigia tecti
ascensu supero atque arrectis auribus asto:
in segetem veluti cum flamma furentibus Austris
incidit, aut rapidus montano flumine torrens   305
sternit agros, sternit sata laeta boumque labores
praecipitesque trahit silvas; stupet inscius alto
accipiens sonitum saxi de vertice pastor.
tum vero manifesta fides, Danaumque patescunt
insidiae. iam Deiphobi dedit ampla ruinam   310
Volcano superante domus, iam proximus ardet
Ucalegon; Sigea igni freta lata relucent.
exoritur clamorque virum clangorque tubarum.
arma amens capio; nec sat rationis in armis,
sed glomerare manum bello et concurrere in arcem   315
cum sociis ardent animi; furor iraque mentem
praecipitat, pulchrumque mori succurrit in armis.

318-67: Aeneas encounters Panthus, a priest of Apollo who has escaped the chaos with his grandson. Panthus reports the general city-wide carnage. Aeneas is again spurred to action and others join him, including Coroebus who is engaged to Cassandra, the priestess daughter of Priam. Aeneas describes death and destruction everywhere.

primus se Danaum magna comitante caterva   370
Androgeos offert nobis, socia agmina credens
inscius, atque ultro verbis compellat amicis:
'festinate, viri! nam quae tam sera moratur
segnities? alii rapiunt incensa feruntque
Pergama: vos celsis nunc primum a navibus itis?'   375

**A
Level**

dixit, et extemplo (neque enim responsa dabantur

fida satis) sensit medios delapsus in hostes.

obstipuit retroque pedem cum voce repressit.

improvisum aspris veluti qui sentibus anguem

pressit humi nitens trepidusque repente refugit   380

attollentem iras et caerula colla tumentem,

haud secus Androgeos visu tremefactus abibat.

inruimus densis et circumfundimur armis,

ignarosque loci passim et formidine captos

sternimus; adspirat primo fortuna labori.   385

atque hic successu exsultans animisque Coroebus

'o socii, qua prima' inquit 'fortuna salutis

monstrat iter, quaque ostendit se dextra, sequamur:

mutemus clipeos Danaumque insignia nobis

aptemus. dolus an virtus, quis in hoste requirat?   390

arma dabunt ipsi.' sic fatus deinde comantem

Androgei galeam clipeique insigne decorum

induitur laterique Argivum accommodat ensem.

hoc Rhipheus, hoc ipse Dymas omnisque iuventus

laeta facit: spoliis se quisque recentibus armat.   395

vadimus immixti Danais haud numine nostro

multaque per caecam congressi proelia noctem

conserimus, multos Danaum demittimus Orco.

diffugiunt alii ad naves et litora cursu

fida petunt; pars ingentem formidine turpi   400

scandunt rursus equum et nota conduntur in alvo.

heu nihil invitis fas quemquam fidere divis!

ecce trahebatur passis Priameia virgo

crinibus a templo Cassandra adytisque Minervae

ad caelum tendens ardentia lumina frustra,   405

lumina, nam teneras arcebant vincula palmas.

non tulit hanc speciem furiata mente Coroebus

et sese medium iniecit periturus in agmen;

consequimur cuncti et densis incurrimus armis.

hic primum ex alto delubri culmine telis   410
nostrorum obruimur oriturque miserrima caedes
armorum facie et Graiarum errore iubarum.
tum Danai gemitu atque ereptae virginis ira
undique collecti invadunt, acerrimus Aiax
et gemini Atridae Dolopumque exercitus omnis: 415
adversi rupto ceu quondam turbine venti
confligunt, Zephyrusque Notusque et laetus Eois
Eurus equis; stridunt silvae saevitque tridenti
spumeus atque imo Nereus ciet aequora fundo.
illi etiam, si quos obscura nocte per umbram   420
fudimus insidiis totaque agitavimus urbe,
apparent; primi clipeos mentitaque tela
agnoscunt atque ora sono discordia signant.
ilicet obruimur numero, primusque Coroebus
Penelei dextra divae armipotentis ad aram   425
procumbit; cadit et Rhipheus, iustissimus unus
qui fuit in Teucris et servantissimus aequi
(dis aliter visum); pereunt Hypanisque Dymasque
confixi a sociis; nec te tua plurima, Panthu,
labentem pietas nec Apollinis infula texit.   430
Iliaci cineres et flamma extrema meorum,
testor, in occasu vestro nec tela nec ullas
vitavisse vices Danaum et – si fata fuissent
ut caderem – meruisse manu. divellimur inde,
Iphitas et Pelias mecum (quorum Iphitas aevo   435
iam gravior, Pelias et vulnere tardus Ulixi),
protinus ad sedes Priami clamore vocati.
hic vero ingentem pugnam, ceu cetera nusquam
bella forent, nulli tota morerentur in urbe,
sic Martem indomitum Danaosque ad tecta ruentes   440
cernimus obsessumque acta testudine limen.
haerent parietibus scalae postesque sub ipsos
nituntur gradibus clipeosque ad tela sinistris

protecti obiciunt, prensant fastigia dextris.
Dardanidae contra turres ac tota domorum   445
culmina convellunt; his se, quando ultima cernunt,
extrema iam in morte parant defendere telis,
aurataque trabes, veterum decora alta parentum,
devolvunt; alii strictis mucronibus imas
obsedere fores, has servant agmine denso.   450
instaurati animi regis succurrere tectis
auxilioque levare viros vimque addere victis.
limen erat caecaeque fores et pervius usus
tectorum inter se Priami postesque relicti,
a tergo infelix qua se, dum regna manebant,   455
saepius Andromache ferre incomitata solebat
ad soceros et avo puerum Astyanacta trahebat.
evado ad summi fastigia culminis, unde
tela manu miseri iactabant inrita Teucri.
turrim in praecipiti stantem summisque sub astra   460
eductam tectis, unde omnis Troia videri
et Danaum solitae naves et Achaica castra,
adgressi ferro circum, qua summa labantes
iuncturas tabulata dabant, convellimus altis
sedibus impulimusque; ea lapsa repente ruinam   465
cum sonitu trahit et Danaum super agmine late
incidit. ast alii subeunt, nec saxa nec ullum
telorum interea cessat genus.
vestibulum ante ipsum primoque in limine Pyrrhus
exsultat telis et luce coruscus aëna: 470
qualis ubi in lucem coluber mala gramina pastus,
frigida sub terra tumidum quem bruma tegebat,
nunc, positis novus exuviis nitidusque iuventa,
lubrica convolvit sublato pectore terga
arduus ad solem, et linguis micat ore trisulcis.   475
una ingens Periphas et equorum agitator Achillis,
armiger Automedon, una omnis Scyria pubes

succedunt tecto et flammas ad culmina iactant.
ipse inter primos correpta dura bipenni
limina perrumpit postesque a cardine vellit   480
aeratos; iamque excisa trabe firma cavavit
robora et ingentem lato dedit ore fenestram.
apparet domus intus et atria longa patescunt;
apparent Priami et veterum penetralia regum,
armatosque videt stantes in limine primo.   485
at domus interior gemitu miseroque tumultu
miscetur; penitusque cavae plangoribus aedes
femineis ululant; ferit aurea sidera clamor.
tum pavidae tectis matres ingentibus errant
amplexaeque tenent postes atque oscula figunt.   490
instat vi patria Pyrrhus; nec claustra nec ipsi
custodes sufferre valent; labat ariete crebro
ianua, et emoti procumbunt cardine postes.
fit via vi; rumpunt aditus primosque trucidant
immissi Danai et late loca milite complent.   495
non sic, aggeribus ruptis cum spumeus amnis
exiit oppositasque evicit gurgite moles,
fertur in arva furens cumulo camposque per omnes
cum stabulis armenta trahit. vidi ipse furentem
caede Neoptolemum geminosque in limine Atridas,   500
vidi Hecubam centumque nurus Priamumque per aras
sanguine foedantem quos ipse sacraverat ignes.
quinquaginta illi thalami, spes tanta nepotum,
barbarico postes auro spoliisque superbi
procubuere; tenent Danai qua deficit ignis.   505
forsitan et Priami fuerint quae fata requiras.
urbis uti captae casum convulsaque vidit
limina tectorum et medium in penetralibus hostem,
arma diu senior desueta trementibus aevo
circumdat nequiquam umeris et inutile ferrum   510
cingitur, ac densos fertur moriturus in hostes.

**A
Level**

aedibus in mediis nudoque sub aetheris axe
ingens ara fuit iuxtaque veterrima laurus
incumbens arae atque umbra complexa penates.
hic Hecuba et natae nequiquam altaria circum, 515
praecipites atra ceu tempestate columbae,
condensae et divum amplexae simulacra sedebant.
ipsum autem sumptis Priamum iuvenalibus armis
ut vidit, 'quae mens tam dira, miserrime coniunx,
impulit his cingi telis? aut quo ruis?' inquit. 520
"non tali auxilio nec defensoribus istis
tempus eget; non, si ipse meus nunc adforet Hector.
huc tandem concede; haec ara tuebitur omnes,
aut moriere simul." sic ore effata recepit
ad sese et sacra longaevum in sede locavit. 525
ecce autem elapsus Pyrrhi de caede Polites,
unus natorum Priami, per tela, per hostes
porticibus longis fugit et vacua atria lustrat
saucius. illum ardens infesto vulnere Pyrrhus
insequitur, iam iamque manu tenet et premit hasta. 530
ut tandem ante oculos evasit et ora parentum,
concidit ac multo vitam cum sanguine fudit.
hic Priamus, quamquam in media iam morte tenetur,
non tamen abstinuit nec voci iraeque pepercit:
'at tibi pro scelere,' exclamat, 'pro talibus ausis 535
di, si qua est caelo pietas quae talia curet,
persolvant grates dignas et praemia reddant debita,
qui nati coram me cernere letum
fecisti et patrios foedasti funere vultus.
at non ille, satum quo te mentiris, Achilles 540
talis in hoste fuit Priamo; sed iura fidemque
supplicis erubuit corpusque exsangue sepulcro
reddidit Hectoreum meque in mea regna remisit.'
sic fatus senior telumque imbelle sine ictu
coniecit, rauco quod protinus aere repulsum, 545

A Level

et summo clipei nequiquam umbone pependit.
cui Pyrrhus: 'referes ergo haec et nuntius ibis
Pelidae genitori. illi mea tristia facta
degeneremque Neoptolemum narrare memento.
nunc morere.' hoc dicens altaria ad ipsa trementem   550
traxit et in multo lapsantem sanguine nati,
implicuitque comam laeva, dextraque coruscum
extulit ac lateri capulo tenus abdidit ensem.
haec finis Priami fatorum, hic exitus illum
sorte tulit Troiam incensam et prolapsa videntem   555
Pergama, tot quondam populis terrisque superbum
regnatorem Asiae. iacet ingens litore truncus,
avulsumque umeris caput et sine nomine corpus.

A
Level

Commentary Notes

'They all fell silent, their gaze fixed on Aeneas.'

*1–39: Aeneas sets the scene. Aeneas grants the request of his host, Queen Dido of Carthage: he will tell the 'unspeakable sorrow' (*infandum ... dolorem 5*) of how Troy fell to the Greek army. He begins with the building of the Wooden Horse, an enormous structure concealing in its 'womb' (*uterumque 20*) an elite squadron of soldiers. He tells how the Greeks packed up and sailed to a nearby island, Tenedos, leaving behind the Horse.*

The Trojans first inspect the abandoned Greek camp and the grim sight of the battlefield. Then they marvel at the Wooden Horse. The structure draws a range of reactions – some are simply gobsmacked; others are instantly suspicious.

40–249: Sinon and Laocoon

40–9: Laocoon attacks the Wooden Horse

40   ibi – The action is still happening outside Troy's walls, near the shore recently abandoned by the Greek army.

41   Laocoon – a brother of Priam and a priest of Neptune or Apollo (201n.). The pleonasm* of **primus ... ante omnes** highlights the urgency of his arrival, and his status quickly attracts an audience (**magna comitante caterva**). This first mention of Laocoon's name (comprising four syllables) is enjambed* to establish his prominence. **ardens** – adverbial: 'desperately'. **arce** – Pergama (n. pl.), the acropolis of Troy.

42   et procul – sc. *poposcit*, or equivalent. The detail suggests Laocoon is hailing a crowd already gathered at the Horse, which contradicts **primus . . . ante omnes 41**. It makes sense to picture a mass descent from the city to the shoreline, led by Laocoon in loud protest.

42   quae tanta insania – sc. *est haec*. The elision running *tanta* into *insania* helps the third and fourth-foot spondees dominate the line and underscore the strength of Laocoon's feeling.

43   avectos hostes – sc. *esse* (often omitted from compound infinitives) in order to complete the indirect statement following *creditis*. In his impassioned state, Laocoon's rhetorical questions fly out as non-standard sentences, lacking interrogatives and/or main verbs.

44   Danaum – contracted *Danaorum*. The alliteration* of **dona . . . dolis . . . Danaum** stresses the core of his warning: the Greeks' gift is all guile. **sic notus Ulixes** – sc. *est vobis*. 'Is Ulysses known to you like this?', meaning they should beware the Greek so notorious for duping his enemy. Laocoon could not have known that Ulysses had not only devised the scheme but was at that moment hidden inside the Horse – and perhaps within earshot: a good example of Virgilian tragic irony.*

45   aut – the second *aut* of four in this speech, each escalating the frustration and disbelief of Laocoon at his peers' naivety. *aut* can mean 'and' as well as 'either/or' in the colloquial dialogue of Roman comedy, especially when linking rhetorical questions. **hoc ligno** – instrumental ablative governed by *occultantur*, lit. 'by this woodwork'; more naturally 'within this woodwork'. Laocoon's choice of **ligno** shows no deference to the structure's potential sanctity. **Achivi** – one of various names Virgil uses for 'Greeks'. Others are *Graii, Danai, Achaei, Achaici, Argolici, Dorici, Pelasgi* – but never *Graeci*.

47   inspectura, ventura – future participles conveying intention. **inspectura** ('to spy on') is a standard verb for military scouts. The

AS

suggestion of Greeks overtopping the city (**desuper**) represents the loss of Troy's strategic advantage. The second action, **ventura**, should logically precede **inspectura**: this is an instance of hysteron proteron,* a disordering device which conveys here the spontaneity and intensity of Laocoon's speech. **urbi** = *in urbem.*

48   **aliquis** – indefinite pronoun used here adjectivally with **error**: 'some other disaster'. **error equo** – this key juxtaposition* is strengthened by the absence of a third-foot caesura, which would put daylight between the two nouns. The accent on **equ-** clashes with the ictus which strikes the -**o**: an ominous jarring on the listener's ear. **ne credite** – a poetic, and archaic,* alternative for *nolite credere.*

49   **et** – adverbial, 'even'. The proper sense of **dona** here is more 'offerings', in a religious context, than 'gifts'.

50   **validis ... viribus** – another instance of pleonasm* which elevates Laocoon. This formula is inherited from Homer, via Ennius, and adds to the image of Laocoon as a warrior-priest in the archaic mould.

51–53   **in latus inque** – with the second **in**, Virgil enlarges the detail of the fateful spear-throw. **curvam** has been transferred to **alvum** from **compagibus**, which it more naturally describes: a not uncommon Virgilianism (cf. **208 immensa volumine terga**). Note the alliteration* here and the emphasis that it lends to the main verb, **contorsit**, when it finally arrives. **alvum** is the first reference to the Horse's anatomy (238n.). Contrast between the bulging 'belly' of soldiers and the hollow ringing of the Horse's flank is tragically ironic.

52   **uteroque recusso** – the sense of *recutio* is 'strike so as to cause to vibrate'. The assonance* in this phrase, as with **insonuere ... dedere** and **cavae ... cavernae** in the line below, effectively enacts the echo of the spear's impact.

AS

53   **insonuere, dedere** – both contracted perfects.

54   **fata deum** – lit. 'what the gods have pronounced'. *fatum*, 'fate', derives from the archaic verb *for, fari, fatus sum*, 'I say'. This original meaning is triggered here, so translate as 'the gods' pronouncements' rather than 'the gods' fates'. **deum** is the archaic form of the classical genitive *deorum* (123n.). Aeneas is speaking now in 'real-time', interrupting his narrative to give the sort of plaintive reflection we might expect from a Greek tragic chorus.

55   **impulerat** – sc. *nos*: 'would have compelled us'. **impulerat** is a rare indicative substitute for the subjunctive usually found in a past-unfulfilled conditional clause. This usage emphasizes just how close Laocoon came to saving the city. **foedare** – a strong, predominantly verse verb meaning 'disfigure, defile'.

56   **staret, maneres** – the imperfect subjunctives express what is, at the time of speaking, now unfulfillable. **maneres**, and the vocative **arx**, constitute a pained apostrophe* to Troy's former citadel.

57–80: Sinon begins his speech

Sinon's entire speech concludes at 194, although it is delivered in four instalments of increasing length (69–72; 76–104; 108–44; 154–94). The questions and comments which mark off each instalment resemble those voiced during a tragic messenger speech (see pp.18–19). The model operates on two levels: Sinon is reporting a catastrophe that has occurred, and he is initiating, by those same words, a greater catastrophe to come.

57   **ecce** – Aeneas conveys his astonishment here as if he were re-enacting the moment Sinon appeared. We could hear this as either performed direct speech or as a narratorial interjection. *ecce* occurs twice as many times in *Aeneid* II as in any other book of the poem (here, 203, 318, 402, 536, 763 and 682); it is a tool used by Virgil to arrest our attention, or dramatically 'cut away' the narrative camera. **manus** – an accusative of respect with **revinctum**: lit. 'tied up [in respect of] his hands'. Translate as if an ablative absolute: *manibus revinctis*. **iuvenem**: the story of Sinon does not derive from Homer, although it is found in the Epic Cycle, and we know that Euripides wrote a tragedy called *Sinon*. **terga** – poetic plural.

58 pastores ... trahebant – a line with the maximum number of spondees (SSSS), conveying the shepherd's strain and Sinon's resistance.

59 Dardanidae – in apposition to **pastores**. *Dardanii* (second declension) and *Dardanidae* (first declension but masculine) are variations of the same royal patronym, applicable to any Trojan, and derived from Troy's second king, Dardanus. **qui** – antecedent is **iuvenem**, not **Dardanidae**. The difficulty of the word order is compounded by the sentence length and by the compression of **venientibus** and **ultro**. It might help to start a new sentence at **qui**, treating it as a connecting relative, 'Sinon, by his own initiative ...'. **venientibus** – 'to them as they approached', meaning the shepherds.

60 hoc ipsum – the object of **strueret**: 'this very thing', i.e., that Sinon would encounter Priam and an audience for his performance.

61 fidens animi – 'trusting in his courage'. **animi** is a genitive of reference, denoting the sphere in which something happens. Not a locative, but resembling one in translation. **utrumque** anticipates the two possibilities contrasted in the line below.

62 seu ... seu. . . – contracted forms of *sive*: 'either ... or'. Here they govern infinitives, rather than the finite verbs usually found in conditionals. That is because the grammatical steer comes from **paratus**, which often takes an infinitive. **versare** – lit. 'to weave, wind, twist', borrowing a Homeric metaphor for the various false narratives 'spun' by Odysseus.

AS

63   visendi studio – lit. 'out of eagerness for spectating'. **studio** is a causal ablative; **visendi** is the dependent gerund. A small detail but, combined with **inludere 64**, it captures the excitable and unguarded mood of the just-liberated Trojans (see pp.13–15).

64   circumfusa – translate as a present participle: 'pouring round'.

65   accipe – With this imperative, Aeneas addresses Dido's request at 1.753f. (*a prima dic, hospes, origine nobis / insidias ... Danaum*). A rare instance during the full narrative where we glimpse her presence (506n.).

66   disce omnes – sc. *insidias*, rather than *Danaos*. This is one of ten unfinished lines (hemistichs) in Book II, more than in any other book. The others are 233, 346, 468, 614, 623, 640, 720, 767 and 787. Virgil died in 19 BC with his manuscript unfinished, but we are told by his fourth-century biographer Aelius Donatus (*Vitae* 32) that Virgil personally recited Books II, IV and VI to Augustus, implying their finished state and/or significance.

67   namque – an explanatory narrative formula ('for indeed') which commonly precedes an *ut*, introducing a temporal clause (*ut* + indicative). **conspectu in medio** – 'in full view'. **turbatus** – a verb favoured by Virgil, used especially of fear, but also of other strong emotions that leave the possessor adrenalized.

68   agmina – a word not uncommon in non-military contexts, especially to denote a jostling crowd.

69   heu – Sinon begins simply, with cautious monosyllables designed to convey distress and bewilderment (cf. **aut quid iam 70**). Sinon wants, firstly, to arouse the Trojans' pity sufficiently to be granted a full hearing. This rhetorical maneouvre, known in Virgil's day as a *commiseratio* (see Cicero's *Rhetorica ad Herennium* 2.31–50), elicits the Trojans' sympathy, but also their curiosity (73–5, 105–7). **quae** –

the interrogative adjective, qualifying **tellus** (f.). The initial sequence of questions sets this speech in the mould of a tragic messenger speech. **restat** – the prefix has an iterative force of 'still'. Taken with **mihi** (dative of disadvantage), an idiomatic English translation would be 'lies in store for me'.

71   cui . . . locus – sc. *est*.

72   poenas cum sanguine – a vague formula which leaves his listeners to assume he means execution. *poena* is usually found in the plural, though we would singularize in English.

73   quo – a connecting relative adjective, qualifying **gemitu**, and referring to all Sinon's outpouring so far: 'by this lament'. **conversi, compressus** – sc. parts of *sum* for these perfect passive indicatives. The *cum-* prefixes hint that the Trojans are vulnerable to herd mentality.

74   hortamur – sc. *eum*. A Virgilian usage of *hortor* with an infinitive, rather than *ut* + subjunctive, for the indirect command. **cretus** – sc. *sit. cretus* is an exclusively verse form; *cresco* in prose is intransitive and lacks a fourth principal part.

75   quidve – 'and what'. The suffix here is an archaism* found in Roman comedy, where *-ve* has been substituted for *-que* after the interrogative *quis, quid* (cf. **aut 45**). **memoret** extends the indirect command following **hortamur**, construed now with the usual subjunctive, and with *ut* omitted. **quae sit fiducia capto** – indirect question containing a possessive dative and the challenge of translating a very Roman abstract noun, **fiducia**. The sense is '[We urged him to state] on what hope he, having been captured, could rely'. **fiducia** is only partially served by 'hope'; its meaning encompasses 'trust, assurance, confidence, reliance'.

76   ille . . . fatur – a line rejected by modern editors as an interpolation. One reason is the detail **deposita . . . formidine** which has struck scholars as inconsistent with the presentation of Sinon so far.

77   rex – an appropriate display of courtesy. This line begins the prefatory Palamedes part of Sinon's story. This section falls in two halves (77–104, then 108–44), each half rising in a crescendo which sustains the curiosity of his audience. **fuerit quodcumque** – future perfect best taken as future simple: 'whatever will come of it'.

78   vera – qualifying **cuncta 77** and delayed for rhetorical effect and to emphasize the predicative sense, 'true as they are'. **neque . . . negabo** – sc. *esse* to complete the indirect statement. The double negative, forming a positive, creates an earnest tone.

79   hoc primum – sc. *est*: 'This is the first thing [to state].' This brief signpost creates a moment of anticipation after Sinon makes his admission of Argive status. Sinon is forthcoming here and in admitting his feud with Ulysses (94–6). This is a disarming strategy whereby he pre-emptively articulates allegations or suspicions which his audience might raise. In Cicero's *De Inventione*, a rhetorical handbook published in the 80s BC, he discusses the skill of *insinuatio* ('ingratiation'): speech which 'sneaks into the listener's sympathies, imperceptibly, by disguise and by circumlocution' (I.20). **miserum Fortuna Sinonem** – Sinon reveals his name using the sort of generalizing observation found in tragic messenger speeches. The third person gives it an air of impartiality; it also helps his generalizing self-characterization. He is one of many simple, innocent folk (like his Trojan audience) who fell victim to Ulysses. **improba** – qualifying **Fortuna** as the subject of **finget**.

81–144: Sinon explains his plight

Sinon's strategy in the next section of speech (76–104) is to arouse Trojan curiosity: he had once enjoyed high status, until he crossed Odysseus and became a target of his cruelty. Sinon appears honourable

AS

in defending the reputation of Palamedes, a relative, and as a victim of Odysseus he finds common ground with the Trojans. Since they accept his characterization of Odysseus, they are ready to accept that the Greeks wanted to abandon Troy and that Odysseus schemed to sacrifice him.

Sinon also appeals to the Trojans' civic values: their sense of family (137–40), their religiousness (141–4) and, later, their concern for the law (155–9): the basic institutions cherished, especially, by survivors of war.

81   fando – an impersonal gerund in the ablative of manner: lit. 'in the telling'. **aliquod** – an adverbial accusative: 'at all'. With the casual **si forte** Sinon keeps up his unassuming persona.

82   Belidae – the patronymic (genitive) of **Palamedis**: 'son of Belus'. The -*i*- of **Belidae** is lengthened for metrical convenience. Virgil departs from earlier accounts of Palamedes' parentage, which record his father as Nauplius. **Palamedis** – a figure from myth whose unjust demise would have been proverbial in Virgil's day. Palamedes exposed Ulysses' attempt to avoid conscription for the Trojan War and in retaliation Ulysses framed Palamedes as a traitor. **fama** – 'in legend'.

83   quem – so begins a syntactically dense section. The skeleton of the relative clause is **quem Pelasgi demisere neci . . . (et quem) nunc lugent. demisere** = *demiserunt*.

84   infando indicio – 'an unspeakable charge', a variation on **falsa sub proditione** in 83. This phrase, preceded by **insontem**, derives additional force from the double elision, the assonance,* and the clash of ictus and accent. **bella** – poetic plural.

85   demisere neci = *demiserunt ad necem*. **nunc**: this is a long and elliptical section, befitting a speaker reliving a painful memory. Translate **quem** again before **nunc. cassum lumine** – sc. *eum*. **lumine** is a poetic usage derived from Homer. It offers Sinon alliteration* and a heightened emotional register. **illi** – dependent on **comitem** and **propinquum. illi**, like **finxit 80**, is a relatively rare self-contained first-foot spondee. An emphatic beginning to the main clause awaited since **si forte 81**.

87   primis . . . ab annis – 'from earliest manhood', i.e., a teenager. If this is true, it seems unlikely he was also leaving behind children, as he claims at 138. This is one of several inconsistencies which the Trojans don't pick up. **pauper** – a pathetic detail which implies financial hardship at home forced him to join the war abroad.

88   stabat – sc. *Palamedes*. **regno incolumis** – 'unchallenged in his kingship'. **regum** – including Palamedes.

89   conciliis – local ablative, with preposition *in* omitted. The enjambment* also emphasizes **vigebat 88**, a simple but expressive verb choice. **et** – adverbial, 'too'. **nos** – poetic plural. **aliquod** qualifies both **nomenque** and **decusque**.

90   gessimus – continuing the poetic plural. The true perfect 'I have carried' implies 'up until now', a forlorn cadence emphasized by enjambment* and the sense-pause after the first dactyl. Austin (1964, p.62): 'one can imagine a sigh'. **invidia** – causal ablative denoting something more active than 'envy': 'malice', or 'spite' perhaps.

91   haud ignota loquor – an aside, strengthened by litotes,* by which Sinon aligns the Trojan perspective with his own: an example of working in small details which cumulatively lend credence to his account and secure what Cicero calls *confirmatio* (*De Inventione* I.24f.). This is when an audience trusts the speaker's corroborating details sufficiently to accept their central argument. **superis . . . ab oris**: lit. 'from the upper shores', meaning the land of the living, that realm situated 'above' the Underworld. A touch of high tragic style (cf. **cassum lumine 85**).

AS

92   in tenebris luctuque – i.e., 'in gloomy grief': an instance of hendiadys* in which one noun, **tenebris**, is concrete and the other abstract. **trahebam** – metaphorical: 'I dragged out'.

93   casum – lit. 'thing that befell him'. Here, and elsewhere in Virgil, it specifically means death. **mecum indignabar** – has a sense of resenting an injustice and grumbling to oneself. **mecum** here, 'within myself'.

94   me – the accusative subject of the indirect statement introduced by **promisi 96**, your starting point as a translator. The implied infinitive is *futurum esse*; **ultorem** modifies **me** predicatively. **fors si qua tulisset** – the first of two conditionals within indirect speech ('sub-oblique'). The pluperfect subjunctives in each (**tulisset, remeassem 95**) would have been future perfects (*tulerit, remeaverim*) in direct speech.

95   remeassem = *remeavissem*. **Argos** – capital of the Argolid, in the north-east Peloponnese. Virgil draws on an unstable mythological record: Palamedes comes from Argos in some versions, from Euboea in others.

96   odia aspera – poetic plural.

97   hinc – the start of a thumping tricolon.* This first *hinc* denotes source: 'from this origin'. The next two are more clearly temporal: 'from this time'. **prima mali labes** – sc. *venit*. **labes** can mean either 'slip, fall', from *labor*, or 'stain', as it means at its other occurrence in the poem (VI.746).

98   terrere, spargere – historic infinitives, along with **quaerere 99**: to be translated as imperfect indicatives. This is a vivid verb form, usually to describe past actions which were either quickly successive or repetitive (cf. 132, 169, 685). Their non-finite-ness spotlights the nature of the action rather than its chronology. **terrere** needs an implied *me*, unless this is deliberate vagueness to suggest Ulysses' blanket brutality.

99   vulgum – not neuter, as more commonly, but masculine. The *-m* ending elides **vulgum** into **ambiguas** and enacts, perhaps, how rumour infiltrated the army. **conscius** – adverbial, 'deliberately'. **arma** – a metonym* referring to the wielders of weapons, as well as their intentions: translate as 'violence' or 'intrigue'.

100   enim – 'in fact', an archaic usage. **Calchante ministro** – Sinon chooses to dramatically break off (aposiopesis*) at the first mention of Calchas, a Greek prophet with an unsavoury reputation. His involvement in the sacrifice of Iphigenia, at the war's outset, and the killing of Astyanax, at its close, would have given his name a disturbing and intriguing ring.

101   sed ... autem – a colloquial doubling of adversative particles. This and other elements of spoken idiom – the repeated **quid,** the **-ve** substitute for **-que** (75n.) – characterize Sinon as authentically spontaneous, like a Greek tragic messenger or an earnest character in Roman comedy. **nequiquam ingrata** – the elision caused by this notable juxtaposition* gives **nequiquam** an appropriately vanishing quality.

102   quidve moror? – 'or why do I bother?' An intransitive usage of *moror* lifted from comedy, where it hovers between 'I've no time for' and 'I'm not fussed'. **uno ordine** – local ablative: 'in the same bracket', i.e., 'alike'.

103   id – i.e., his Greek identity. **sat est** = *satis est vobis.* **iamdudum sumite poenas** – **iamdudum** is an idiomatic adverb compressing reference to both past and present time. The sense is '*now* exact the punishment *long since due*'.

104   Ithacus – Sinon continues to fuel Trojan antipathy towards Ulysses. **velit, mercentur** – main clause 'potential' subjunctives. The present tense refers to future time: 'he would wish', 'they would purchase'. **magno** – ablative of price asked or paid: 'at a high price'. The

AS

idiom leaves *pretio* understood. **Atridae** – the sons of Atreus, i.e.,
Agamemnon and Menelaus, who led the Greek forces at Troy.

105 tum vero – a phrase used here and elsewhere (228, 309) to
signal a critical juncture in the narrative. **scitari** – an iterative deponent
form of *scio*, governed by **ardemus**, and with *cuncta* or *multa*
understood as its object.

107 pavitans – 'fearful'. Fear both feigned and also, one might
suggest, real. **ficto pectore** – here, as often, *pectus* is used for the seat
of emotions. There is another tense ambiguity: Sinon must outwardly
rehearse the right emotions and he must privately steel himself.

108 Troia … relicta – a plausible fabrication (91n.). In the *Iliad*,
Agamemnon moots the prospect of abandoning Troy in order to
test his troops (*Il.* II.73–181), and Achilles, the Greeks' best
fighter, repeatedly threatens an early exit (e.g., IX.412–16). **cupiere** =
cupiverunt.

109 moliri – deponent, taking **fugam 108** as its object: 'to accomplish
their retreat'. The verb implies pulling off a complex feat despite
adverse conditions.

110 fecissentque utinam – Sinon allows himself a moment of
theatrical parenthesis, emphatically promoting the verb before
utinam. The pluperfect 'optative' subjunctive expresses a past
unfulfilled wish. **saepe** – resuming, rhetorically, **saepe 108**. This
sentence is longer than it needs to be, but it is important for Sinon to
labour this weather detail because it serves to corroborate (in the
Trojans' eyes) his key claim: that the Greeks wanted to leave, and have
left. **Auster** – a southerly wind which would frustrate a ship sailing
south from the Troad (304n.). **euntes** – 'as they set out'.

112 praecipue cum iam hic – Sinon now gives the Horse its first
mention. The detail feels somewhat incidental, given the structure's

AS

hulking presence and Laocoon's warning. Sinon takes care to slip it casually into the longer account of weather problems. Note the distance of **equus 113** from its adjective: the Horse is initially just **hic**, 'this thing'.

113   toto . . . aethere – *in* is usually omitted from phrases containing *totus*, in verse and prose.

114   scitatum – the supine of *scitor*. Following a verb of motion (**mittimus 115**) the accusative supine expresses purpose: 'in order to ask'. **oracula** – poetic plural. Likely Apollo's oracle at Thymbra (near Troy) or Grynium (further down the Turkish coast), rather than Delphi. **Phoebus** is a poetic appellation for Apollo as the god of light (Greek Φοῖβος, 'radiant, bright').

115   adytis – ablative of separation, in the poetic plural. The *adytum* was the inner room of a temple or shrine.

116   placastis = *placavistis*. **virgine caesa** – instrumental ablative like **sanguine**: 'through a girl slaughtered', i.e., by the killing of Iphigenia, the daughter of Agamemnon sacrificed at Aulis in return for favourable winds.

117   Iliacas – a synonym for *Troianus*. In Latin, Troy is known as both *Troia* (after the founding king, Tros) and *Ilium* (after its second king, Ilios).

118   sanguine mirrors 116 and reinforces, on the ear, the parallelism of the oracle's response. **quaerendi, litandum** – gerundives of obligation with *sunt* and *est* understood. **quaerendi** modifies **reditus**, whereas **litandum** is used impersonally: lit. 'there is to be an obtaining of favourable omens'. **reditus** – poetic plural. The abstract noun and the symmetrical word order gives the oracle a grandly indefinite tone: another detail to reel in Sinon's audience.

119   Argolica – strategically delayed. Sinon chooses the synonym for 'Greek' which derives from his own home region (**Argos 95**) because he knows that his captivated audience will catch the clue to whose life (**anima**) will be at stake. **quae** – connecting relative adjective with **vox**, the subject of the temporal **ut** clause: 'this speech'.

121   cui fata parent, quem poscat Apollo – indirect questions dependent on an understood verb of thought, e.g., *meditantes* or (*secum*) *volventes*. The absence of an object for **parent** is initially awkward but in fact adds, by ellipsis, to the sinister vagueness of what impends. Translate as 'make preparations' to avoid stilted English.

122   Calchanta – Greek accusative singular. **hic** – temporal, not spatial: 'at this moment'.

123   in medios – sc. *eos*. **quae sint ea numina divum** – indirect question governed by **flagitat** in the line below: 'he demanded [to know] what in this case was the will of the gods'. *numen* is plural for singular and **divum** is an old genitive plural form.

124   canebant – here a synonym for *praedico*, with an inceptive force: 'began to predict'.

125   artificis – i.e., Ulysses. **et taciti** – likely a different group to the **multi** of 124, who had voiced their reactions in **canebant**. Some onlookers, we infer, actively expressed concern; others were too relieved to offer support and risk the attention of Calchas. **ventura** – neuter accusative plural of *venturus*, here used substantively with a non-literal sense: 'what would transpire'.

126   bis quinos ... dies – 'for ten days'. An epic periphrasis which combines the numeral adverb *bis* ('two times') with the distributive adjective *quinus* ('five each'), here standing in for *quinque*. **ille** – i.e., Calchas, who broods on the oracle's response (**silet ... tectus**) before condemning Sinon: a relatively incidental, but dramatic, detail.

AS

127   aut – connecting **opponere** and **prodere**, rather than posing them as alternatives (45n.).

128   vix tandem – 'finally, scarcely', meaning with (feigned) reluctance. Sinon's teasing aposiopesis* at line 100 (**Calchante ministro**) has us guessing as to Calchas's character and crime. His initial conduct, however, seems quite innocent: he only participates at Ulysses' insistence (**protrahit 123**). That discrepancy, the hint of duplicity, is what sustains the story and, ironically, secures for Sinon his audience's attention.

129   rumpit vocem – 'he broke his silence': an idiom coined by Virgil after Greek usage, in which the sound that breaks the silence (**vocem**) is made the object of the verb. Calchas' duplicity is now exposed. The force of **rumpit** and the elision of **vocem et** suggest a swift, damning manoeuvre.

130   adsensere = *adsenserunt*. **quae** – sc. the antecedent *ea*, qualified by **conversa 131**. Take **conversa** as 'when exchanged', with the sense of something undesirable being deflected onto someone else. The other men tolerated '*what things* each was fearing for himself, *when exchanged*'.

131   unius in miseri exitium – 'for the death of a single man'. **tulere** = *tulerunt*: 'permitted, tolerated'. The sense of 130–1 is that the Greek collective who had feared the *prospect* of a human sacrifice, accepted the *outcome* of Sinon's selection (i.e., someone else's poor luck).

Moments like this in the Sinon–Laocoon episode form part of an extended psychological commentary on what happens when crowds hear words: the crowd of Greeks in Sinon's tale; the crowd of Trojans watching Sinon; the Carthaginians hearing Aeneas; and the *plebs Romana* of recent Roman history, responding to political rhetoric.

132   dies infanda – i.e., the day of his death. **dies** is here feminine rather than masculine, as at 126, to denote an appointed day. **sacra** – a substantive neuter plural from *sacer*: 'sacrificial things, rites'. **parari** – historic infinitive (98n.).

133   salsae fruges et circum tempora vittae: the sundries of an animal sacrifice. Salt and grain would be sprinkled on the victim's head, on the altar and even on the knives. *vittae* were woollen bands which secured thick plaited garlands (*infulae*) on the heads of both priest and victim.

134   leto – 'from death'. After a verb of *taking away* (**eripui**), Latin has a dative indirect object rather than an ablative of separation.

135   limosoque lacu – local ablative, 'by a slimy lake'. **obscurus** – 'hidden', but belonging more naturally with **noctem**, an instance of hypallage.* Sinon's atmospheric (onomatopoeic?) description helps to distract from the minimal detail of his escape.

136   dum … darent – 'until they should set sail'. The subjunctive adds an element of purpose to the temporal clause: he hid until they had sailed away, removing the danger. The *dum* and *si* clauses give Sinon's rationale as if an implied indirect statement: 'I hid, until [*so I thought*] they … reckoned that …'. This explains the mood and tense of **dedissent**: a direct speech future perfect (*dederint*).

137   mihi iam … spes ulla – sc. *est*. Sinon prepares us for the emotional *commiseratio* (69n.) of **141** with the intensifying touches of **iam** and **ulla**, which often embellish moments of Virgilian pathos. **videndi** – genitive gerund dependent on **spes**. In verse, gerunds are freer to take a direct object (**patriam**).

138   natos – 87n.

139   illi – i.e., the Greeks. **fors et** – both words adverbial, 'maybe even': a Virgilian idiom.

AS

140 **effugia** – poetic plural. **culpam hanc** – the postponed **hanc** acquires additional demonstrative force through elision here. **miserorum** – i.e., Sinon's family: a reiteration of line 138's pathetic detail.

141 **quod** – adverbial, used in conversation to transition between sentences: translate as 'now' or 'well'. **te** – accusative object of **oro 143**. **per superos et conscia numina veri** – *per*, here 'by', is the preposition for invocations. **veri** is dependent on **conscia numina**: 'divine powers knowing of truth'. A disingenuous variation on the solemn phrase *conscia sidera testor* used elsewhere in the poem by characters in distress (e.g., Dido IV.519).

142 **si qua . . . fides** – the whole *si* clause here, including its relative clause (**quae restet**), acts as an accusative object of the second **per**. Take **si qua** (lit. 'if any') as 'whatever'. **restet** – a generic subjunctive, found in relative clauses with indefinite antecedents.

143 **miserere laborum** – second singular imperative of *misereor*, which takes an objective genitive: 'have pity of [i.e. *for*] . . .'. The repetition of **miserere** and the enjambed assonance* of **laborum/ tantorum** bring Sinon's appeal to an effective climax.

145–94: Sinon explains the Wooden Horse

Once Sinon has secured the Trojans' trust and dispatched their suspicions, he can deliver the critical, but more complex, content: what the Horse signifies. Again, he uses the offensive behaviour of Ulysses to lend credibility to his explanation: Ulysses stole the sacred Palladium of Troy and as recompense Athena demanded an expiatory offering – the Wooden Horse. He must also explain the size of the Horse: it is large so that the Trojans cannot wheel it into their city and win Athena's goodwill for themselves. By this point, Sinon has the

Trojans in the palm of his hand and we find it entirely believable that they should accept his explanation of the Horse.

145 his lacrimis – the indirect object of **damus**, rather than ablative of time or cause: 'we granted his life [in response] to these tears'. Aeneas, narrating in retrospect, emphasizes the emotional impact of Sinon's present histrionics rather than the past misfortune. As emotion intensifies on the Trojan side, Sinon is able to compose himself for the key objective: explaining the Horse.

146 ipse viro primus – Priam takes charge decisively (and voluntarily, **ultro 145**) as the word order suggests. **viro** dignifies Sinon (vs. *ei*) and anticipates the eager generosity of **noster eris 149**. **primus . . . iubet** – 'he was the first to order'.

149 noster eris – a two-word parenthesis which conveys Priam's humaneness and Sinon's achievement. **haec** – accusative object of **roganti**, looking ahead to the fast flight of questions.

150 quo – 'for what purpose', introducing the first of five direct questions in two lines: an energetic burst like no other in the poem. The pace of questioning hikes the tempo after Sinon's circuitous speech and reflects the excitable state of the Trojans. **statuere** = *statuerunt*. **quis auctor?** – sc. *est*, as for **quae religio** and **quae machina 151**. **religio** – 'religious duty', something one is bound to observe (*ligo*, 'I bind').

151 quidve – 75n. **quae machina belli?** – Laocoon's word at 47. This question credits Priam with more wariness than might appear initially.

152 dixerat – a common verse usage of the pluperfect to mark that, now the speech has concluded, the narrative can resume. **arte Pelasga** – amplifying **dolis** but also evoking **106**: a detail which keeps in view the narrator, Aeneas, and his evaluative filter.

153 vinclis – ablative of separation: 'from his bonds'.

AS

154   vos, aeterni ignes – vocative address to the sun, moon and stars: a dramatic opening to the preamble (154–61) of Sinon's concluding speech (154–94). **non violabile** – a Virgilian coinage, creating by litotes* a variation on the usual *inviolabilis*. The positive form of the adjective also enforces by alliteration* the frame of **vos** and **vestrum**.

155   nefandi – a loose personification* of **enses**, insinuating the foul intentions of Calchas and Ulysses rather than the invoked gods.

156   hostia – in apposition to the implied subject of **gessi**, Sinon: 'as a sacrificial victim'.

157   fas – sc. *sit* (jussive subjunctive) rather than *est*. We should hear Sinon's words as tentative and god-fearing, rather than presumptuous. **fas,** along with **iura** and **legibus 159**, belongs to the realm of Roman law and the religious observance which governed legal ethics. *fas* is neuter, indeclinable and only used predicatively to modify another noun, often the infinitive (a verbal noun). **fas** (*sit*) **mihi** – 'let it be right for me to ...'. **Graiorum** – 'oaths of the Greeks', possessed by them (subjective genitive) and imposed on him.

158   sub auras – 'out into the open'.

159   qua – an alternative for *quae* (accusative plural) for the neuter indefinite pronoun: 'if they are concealing *any things*'.

160   tu – an apostrophe* to **Troia 161**, rather than the Trojans: an appropriately dramatic flourish to end this section. **promissis** – a local ablative but more naturally translated, with **maneas**, by 'let you stick *to* your promises'. **maneas, serves** – jussive subjunctives. The polyptoton* of **servataque serves** ramifies the tragic irony* that the Trojans, by exhibiting **fidem**, will in fact betray themselves. Cf. the ironic ambiguity of **si magna rependam 161**.

162 omnis spes Danaum – Priam's questions are side-stepped as Sinon begins another winding narrative, again starting from a known event: the theft of Athena's Palladium. His task is to connect convincingly the indisputable disappearance of one talisman with the suspicious appearance of another, the Horse. **fiducia** – 75n.

163 Palladis – Pallas is an epithet of Athena which, by this time, was used on its own to denote the goddess of war who brandished (Greek πάλλω) a shield and spear. **auxiliis** – local ablative. Athena's support for the Greeks over the Trojans, who tragically revered her nonetheless, ended when Ajax (414n.) assaulted her priestess Cassandra (403–15). **ex quo** – sc. *tempore*. A correlative unit completed by **ex illo 169**: 'from the time when … from that time …'.

164 Tydides – patronym of Diomedes, son of Tydeus and a Greek commander at Troy. **sed enim** – 100n.

165 fatale – 'fateful', in the sense that Troy's fortunes resided with the Palladium (166n). **adgressi** – meaning 'daring to' when followed by an infinitive.

166 Palladium – a wooden statue of Athena described by Pseudo-Apollodorus (first/second century AD) as similar to a Greek *kore*, 1.37m tall, with a spear in one hand and weaving apparatus in the other. An oracle had declared that Troy would survive while the icon lived within its walls.

167 corripuere = *corripuerunt*.

168 ausi – sc. *sunt*. **contingere** – with polluting connotations. That Ulysses and Diomedes defiled the statue so carelessly is one of Sinon's less plausible details.

169 fluere, referri – historic infinitives (98n.), governed by **170 spes** and best treated as perfect indicatives.

AS

170   **fractae, aversa** – sc. parts of *sum* to produce perfect passive indicatives.

171   **nec dubiis . . . monstris** – take **nec** with **dubiis** rather than **dedit**. **Tritonia** – i.e., Athena. This cult-title derives from the ancient river Triton in Tunisia (near modern Al-Hammah), which was claimed as the site of Athena's 'birth' from her father's head. **ea signa** – i.e., indications of Athena's *mens aversa*.

172   **vix positum** – sc. *est*. The **vix** leads us to expect an inverse *cum* clause ('this had hardly happened, *when . . .*'), but the sudden arrival of **arsere** (=*arserunt*) defies that possibility. A dramatic example of parataxis* supporting the poem's content. **castris** – local ablative.

173   **luminibus . . . arrectis** – *lumen* a common poetic synonym for *oculus*. *arrigo* is often found in a context of danger (cf. 206, of the sea-snakes). **luminibus** and **solo 174** both denote place 'from where' (sc. *e*). **salsus . . . sudor** – a typical Roman phenomenon when statues express their gods' displeasure. Sinon gives this scene all the trappings of a conventional prodigy report.

174   **mirabile dictu** – '[a thing] astonishing to report'. **mirabile** is in the accusative, the case of exclamations in Latin; **dictu** is the ablative supine of *dico*: lit. 'by the act of telling'.

176   **temptanda . . . aequora** – sc. *esse* for the indirect statement following **canit. fuga** – 'in flight'.

177   **Pergama** – the next accusative subject of the indirect statement, here governing **posse** (41n).

178   **omina ni repetant** – 'unless they were to seek new auspices'. **ni** is a contracted form of *nisi*. The present subjunctive **repetant** follows the strict sequence determined by **canit**, which is (historic) present. **Argis** – locative usage: 'in Argos'.

AS

179 **pelago** – ablative of extension: 'across the sea' (cf. 528). **avexere** = *avexerunt*. The relative clause (**quod . . . carinis**) belongs to Sinon (direct speaker) rather than Calchas (indirect), which accounts for the indicative **avexere**. It is left unclear why the Greeks had taken the Palladium back with them to Greece when they sought new omens.

180 **quod** – adverbial, connecting sections of speech: 'as to the fact that'. **vento petiere Mycenas** – **vento** instrumental ablative modifying **petiere** (= *petiverunt*). Mycenae was Agamemnon's citadel in the Argolid.

181 **comites** – in apposition to **deos**: 'as comrades'. **pelagoque remenso** – ablative absolute: the perfect participle of *remetior* can be active or passive, as here.

182 **aderunt** – 'they will be upon us': an understated verb, and tragically ironic.* The dactyls and elision of the line's first half support the sense with a quick tempo.

183 **hanc . . . effigiem** – since its last mention, Priam's question at 150, the Horse has become an *effigies*, like the Palladium (167), rather than an *equus*.

184 **nefas quae triste piaret** – relative clause with subjunctive to convey purpose: 'which may [= so that it may] expiate the wretched wrongdoing'.

185 **tamen** –modifying the second instruction of Calchas: build a Horse offering, *but* build it tall enough that the Trojans cannot claim it for their city. **attollere** – sc. *nos* to complete the indirect command introduced by **iussit 186**. **immensam** modifies **molem** predicatively: 'raise high this structure here' rather than 'raise this high structure here'.

186 **roboribus textis** – 'with interlocking timbers'. *robur* usually means oak, but Virgil also builds his Horse from fir (*abiete* 16), maple (**acernis 112**) and pine (*pinea* 258), and rarely resorts to the less poetic

AS

lignum. tego is a common verb for elaborate joinery. **caeloque educere** = *in caelum educere.*

188   neu – contracted form of *neve* (= *et ne*). **antiqua sub religione** – referring to the ancient reciprocal obligations observed by Athena and the Trojans: they worshipped the goddess, and so she (i.e., the Palladium) watched over Troy. Sinon deftly suggests the just-lost Palladium and the just-found Horse are two equivalent talismans.

189   vestra manus – singular for plural. **violasset** = *violavisset.* 189–94 are the reported warning of Calchas, introduced by an implicit *monuit.* The syntactical symmetry (a pair of conditionals – **si, sin**) gives these lines an oracular tone (118n.). The two pluperfect subjunctives (**violasset, ascendisset**) represent direct speech future perfects; the future infinitives (**futurum, venturam** – sc. *esse*) represent future simple main verbs. **dona** – poetic plural.

190   tum magnum exitium – **tum** is more demonstrative (like *ita*) than temporal. This is the only instance of three consecutive *-um* words in Virgil. The assonance* here and in the line below (**ipsum, futurum**) lends an ominous weight to Sinon's warning. **quod** – modifies **omen** as a relative adjective: 'this omen'. **di** = *dei.* **convertant** – jussive subjunctive. This parenthesis aligns Sinon with the Trojans, wishing **exitium** on Calchas (**in ipsum**).

191   Phrygibus – i.e., the Trojans. Phrygia was the wider region of Asia Minor in which Troy sat.

192   vestris vestram – the alliteration* in 191–4 elevates the diction of Calchas: convincing mimicry on Sinon's part. **ultro** – Troy, 'going further still', will actually bring war to Greece. **Asiam** = *Troiam.* This is *Asia* in the limited, Homeric usage as opposed to the entire continent of Asia, which it does mean elsewhere in the *Aeneid.* **Pelopea ad moenia** – an exalted periphrasis for *ad Graeciam.* Pelops was the grandfather of Agamemnon and Menelaus and founder of the semi-historical Pelopid dynasty which ruled much of the Peloponnese ('the island of Pelops').

195–227: The death of Laocoon

Laocoon is the only Trojan to cast aspersions on the Horse, but he is also tragically powerless to win round a crowd which Sinon has disarmed. In Sinon's success we observe what happens when a skilful speaker is able to manipulate an anxious crowd into acting against their own interests. Such a group dynamic would have been familiar to those who had lived through the populism of the late Republic.

195   talibus insidiis ... arte – causal ablatives: 'through such deception and through the skill'. Aeneas breaks off his narrative to evaluate the story so far and prepare us for the now-anticipated death of Laocoon.

196   credita res – sc. *est*. Here *credo* is used transitively in the sense of 'believe true'. Sinon's tale has been accepted by the Trojans; Laocoon's death will provide the confirmation they need to act. **capti** – sc. *sumus*. The implicit subject *nos* should be understood as the antecedent of **quos 197. lacrimisque coactis** – i.e., crocodile tears (145n.).

197   Larisaeus – Larissa was the capital of Achilles' homeland in eastern Thessaly.

198   domuere = *domuerunt*. Aeneas' list of what did *not* undo the Trojans is an inversion of the *priamel*, a rhetorical pattern which climactically reveals something by first dismissing some alternatives. 'Troy fell not because of A, or B, or C, but because of D.' **mille carinae** – the round number inherited from Virgil's poetic antecedents, beginning with Aeschylus' *Agamemnon*.

AS

199   hic – temporal (122n.). **miseris** – sc. *nobis*. **multo** is an ablative
of the measure of difference: 'by much', modifying the comparative
phrase **tremendum ... magis** ('more dreadful'). *tremendus* is the
gerundive of *tremo*, and as a verb form it uses the periphrasis *magis* +
adjective instead of a comparative inflection (*-ior/-ius*).

201   Laocoon – Laocoon reappears in a different location by a
narrative sleight of hand. Either he has shunned the crowd and
the captive, or he has listened tight-lipped to Sinon's speech: neither
seems plausible. **Neptuno** – other versions of Laocoon's death
identify him as a priest of Apollo. It is conceivable he has association
with more than one cult, given his royal status (41n.). What is
significant here is that he is no longer acting as prince (40–53) but
as priest.

202   sollemnes – originally *sollemnis*, derived from *annus*, meant
'regular, yearly'. There is a sense of that here: Laocoon is observing a
customary and timely ritual. The purpose of the sacrifice is not given,
but **sollemnes**, the bull, and the spondees all indicate an important
occasion. **ad aras** – plural for singular.

203   a Tenedo – the Turkish island of Bozcaada, sixteen miles south-
west of Troy, where the Greek army was lying in wait. **alta** – poetic
plural (lit. 'the depths').

204   horresco referens – a tense narratorial parenthesis which
dramatically delays the subject of these lines, **angues. immensis
orbibus** – ablative of description.

205   pelago – indirect object of **incumbunt**, lit. 'they lean upon the
sea'. Water snakes propel themselves forward by unilaterally
contracting and expanding their bellies (see YouTube). Virgil's verb
choice vividly captures how the snakes exert themselves without
disturbing the sea's surface.

AS

206   pectora quorum – postponed connecting relative (antecedent **angues**): 'their breasts'. **arrecta** – sc. *sunt*. The alliteration* within **inter fluctus arrecta** suggests alert and coordinated movement. Cf. **pelago pariterque 205** and **sanguineae superant**.

207   pars cetera – i.e., what, of their body, was not considered head/crest. **pontum legit** – lit. 'picks [a path through] the sea': an idiom of high epic, used elsewhere of ships.

208   immensa volumine terga – **terga** is a common plural for singular – although here it does add to the snakes' monstrous size (cf. **immensis 204, arrecta 206, superant 207**). See 51n. for the transferral of **immensa** from the ablative **volumine**.

209   spumante salo – instrumental ablative rather than ablative absolute; **salo** is an epic synecdoche* for '(salt-)sea'. **arva tenebant** – lit. 'they held the fields', meaning 'they were traversing land'. It actually makes more sense for the land to temporarily 'hold' the snakes, but their relentless movement keeps them in control, grammatically.

210   ardentesque oculos suffecti sanguine et igni – 'their blazing eyes shot through with blood and fire'. An example of a passive participle (**suffecti**) 'retaining' the accusative (**oculos**) which, in an active form, it would have governed as a direct object. This is a poetic construction with participles that can carry a reflexive sense: lit. 'having steeped themselves [reflexive] their eyes [accusative retained] with blood and fire [ablative]'.

212   visu exsangues – 'made pale by the sight of it'. **visu** is a causal ablative modifying **exsangues**, an especially vivid adjective in the context of **sanguineae 207, sanguine 210** and **sanie 221. agmine certo** – ablative of manner.

213   Laocoonta – Greek accusative singular, dramatically enjambed.* The strong pause after **petunt** gives additional weight to this first mention of the snakes' victim. **amplexus** – perfect participles of deponent verbs can often, as here, carry a continuous sense: '[embraced and continued] embracing'.

215 implicat – lit. 'folds in'. The pacing of this line clarifies the action: in two initial dactyls the children are easily captured; then a momentary pause at the third-foot caesura; then the snakes take two spondees to chew down their prey, as slowly and precisely as **depascitur** implies. **post** – adverb, balancing **et primum 213.**

216 auxilio – dative of purpose, 'to help', after a verb of motion (**subeuntem**).

218 medium – 'his torso', which the elision 'feeds' to the snakes (**amplexi**). **collo squamea circum terga dati** – *circumdo* often has the encircling item (**squamea . . . terga**) as direct object and the encircled (**collo**) as indirect object, as here. **circum . . . dati** = *circumdati*, a splitting up (*tmesis*) not uncommon with a disyllabic prefix. The voice of the participle is here closer to the Greek middle ('having got their scaly bodies around') but translate as if active: 'having encircled his neck with their scaly bodies'.

219 superant – sc. *eum.*

220 simul – in tandem with **simul 222**: 'while . . . at the same time . . .'.

221 perfusus sanie vittas – a retained accusative phrase (210n.). *sanies*, strictly meaning 'putrid blood', is a lurid synonym for *sanguis.*

223 quales mugitus – This is a highly compressed, correlative construction which picks up **clamores 222**: '[*tales*] *clamores tollit quales mugitus taurus* [*dat*] *cum . . .*' ('he raised such cries as what bellows a bull gives when . . .'). A literal sacrifice becomes figurative, and Laocoon's priestly *vittae* become the garlands of a victim (133n.). **fugit** – long -*u*- and so perfect tense.

224 **cervice** – ablative of separation, following **excussit. securim** – *securis* has accusative singular -*im* and ablative singular -*i*, as does *turris*, 'tower' (460).

225 **at** – the only indication that Laocoon's fierce resistance could not save him. **lapsu** – ablative of manner: 'by slithering off'. **delubra ad summa** – i.e., the temple of Athena on Troy's citadel. A *delubrum* was originally where water was stored for ritual purification; here, it is a synonym for 'temple'.

226 **Tritonidis** – 171n. The poem (or Aeneas?) leaves us – along with the Trojans – to infer that Laocoon died because he threatened to expose the Horse and jeopardize the victory of Athena's Greeks. **deae** – i.e., the goddess' cult statue.

227 **sub ... sub ...** – the repetition of **sub** and -**que** conveys the snakes slithering out of sight, one after the another, down to a dark recess.

228–49: The Wooden Horse enters Troy

Once the Trojans have accepted Sinon's explanation of the Horse (*credita res* 196), it will take only a small leap of logic for them to interpret Laocoon's mysterious death as divine retribution for attacking Athena's Horse.

The Horse enters over twelve lines laden with tragic irony as the Trojans celebrate, oblivious to what awaits them. Aeneas' anguish as he remembers the event (241–2) recalls a tragic chorus expressing horror at what has happened or will happen.

228 **tum vero** – a favourite formula of Virgil for signalling a climax: cf. 105, 309. **tremefacta ... per pectora** – *pectus* was the seat of feelings, as at 107 and 200. The Trojans are jittery having seen grim confirmation of what Sinon convincingly explained. **cunctis** – dative of disadvantage: translate as if genitive.

229   scelus – an object of both the predicative participle **merentem**, qualifying **Laocoonta**, and the infinitive **expendisse**.

It is worth asking why Aeneas excludes himself from the main verbs **ferunt 230, conclamant 233, accingunt 235, subiciunt 236** and **intendunt 237**, but includes himself in **dividimus** and **pandimus 234**. See 'Narratorial standpoint', pp.10–13.

230   sacrum ... robur – i.e., the Horse (186n.).

231   laeserit, intorserit – subjunctives for a sub-oblique relative clause, with an added causal flavour: Laocoon pays the price 'as one who [= because he] violated ... hurled'. **tergo** – indirect object of **intorserit. sceleratam** – a transferred epithet: the crime is Laocoon's, not the spear's. Virgil gives us this scene through the eyes of the alarmed Trojans (focalization). The spear-cast was 'criminal', and the Horse is 'holy' only because they have interpreted Laocoon's death in light of Sinon's story.

232   ducendum, orandaque – sc. *esse*. **ad sedes** – both **sedes** (here, 'temple') and **numina 233** govern **divae**, a subjective genitive. **simulacrum** – i.e., the Horse, a large-scale copy (*simulo* – I imitate) of an actual horse.

233   numina – plural for singular, here meaning 'goodwill, grace'. This is an unfinished line which, like **66**, seems to cliff-hang quite effectively.

234   dividimus – a significant switch to the first-person (cf. 105, 145). **muros et moenia** – an alliterative* pair which expands a single, very significant, action to the length of a whole line. Take **moenia** as 'fortified ramparts' (*munio* – I fortify).

235   operi – indirect object of **accingunt**: 'they ply themselves *at the task*'. It is ambiguous as to whether Aeneas includes himself among

omnes (229n.). **rotarum/lapsus** – lit. 'glidings of wheels', a Virgilian invention for 'wheeled platform'. There is an ominous echo here (and in **inlabitur 240**) of the snakes' **lapsu** at 225.

236 collo – indirect object of **intendunt**: 'they lead [ropes] *around its neck*'.

237 scandit – the standard verb for scaling a city wall, and so a subtle personification* of the Horse: now animate, it governs the main verb and rumbles in over four strenuous spondees. **fatalis machina muros** – an ironic echo of Laocoon's **machina muros 46**.

238 feta armis – lit. 'pregnant with weapons', resuming the metaphor* already active (20, 38, 52) and continued in **utero 243**.

239 sacra – sc. *carmina*. Celebrant children, hymns, ropes and decorative greenery (**festa ... fronde 249**) all belong to Roman ritual processions, occasions which often mark continuity (rather than calamity).

240 illa – i.e., the Horse. **mediaeque ... urbi** – dative expressing motion towards, after **inlabitur**.

241 o patria, o divum domus – an emotive pair of exclamations, and a pre-emptive epitaph for a city which, despite its temples (**domus divum**) and tall walls (**moenia Dardanidum**), must fall. **domum** is in apposition to **Ilium**.

242 quater – a variation on *ter*, the usual number of bad omens.

244 caecique furore – the *furor* here is an extension of **immemores**: the folly of humans being ignorant or incautious. The Trojans have fatally underestimated the treachery of Greeks and misinterpreted Laocoon's death.

245 monstrum – here more 'monstrosity' than 'warning sign' (171).

246 **fatis aperit Cassandra futuris / ora** – lit. 'Cassandra opened her lips for what fates were to come. **fatis ... futuris** is a dative of purpose. Cassandra was a daughter of Priam who rejected Apollo (**dei 247**) and as punishment received the gift of prophecy but the curse of never being believed.

247 **credita Teucris** – plausibly qualifying both **ora** *and* **Cassandra**. *Teucri* is Virgil's commonest word for 'Trojans' and refers to the first king of Troy, Teucer. **Teucris** is a dative of agent, an alternative to the ablative (after *a/ ab*) and found especially with gerundives and passive participles, as here. **credita** – the transitive usage of *credo* (196n.).

248 **deum** = *deorum*. **quibus ultimus esset / ille dies** – the subjunctive **esset** gives this relative clause a concessive sense: 'we, poor souls, decked the temples ... we for whom [even though] it was the last day'.

250–67: Sinon lets the Greek army into Troy. As soon as night falls, the Greek fleet sails back from its concealed mooring off Tenedos. Sinon unbolts the Wooden Horse and releases into Troy an elite unit of Greek soldiers. They slaughter the guards at the city gates, and the rest of the Greek army soon floods into a city 'buried' (sepultum) by wine and sleep.

268–317: Hector and Aeneas

268–80 The ghost of Hector

The ghost of Hector appears to Aeneas in a dream. Aeneas, bewildered, tries to engage the ghost with questions (281–6). Hector enjoins Aeneas to flee: Troy is finished and Aeneas is destined to save the city's gods and seek out 'great walls' (287–97).

It is Troy's religious identity, embodied by its *penates*, which Hector urges Aeneas to preserve. In Book III (143–71), the city's gods will themselves visit Aeneas in a dream.

268   quo – ablative time when: '[it was the time] **when** …'. After the previous night's celebration, we are now in the small hours of the next day.

269   dono divum – 'by the gods' good grace': an alliterative* formula and something of a cliché, but here it adds to the lulled atmosphere.

270   in somnis – poetic plural. **ecce** – (57n.). The pathos of this section comes from the tragic contrast between Trojan repose and Greek impetus; between Hector once distinguished and now disfigured; and between Aeneas's foggy interaction with Hector and the painful clarity of his hindsight. **Hector** – Priam bore fifty sons but Hector was first in line and held overall command of Troy's army. He met his match in Achilles, who in *Iliad* XXII kills him in retaliation for the death of Patroclus (275n.). The visit of Patroclus' ghost to Achilles at *Il.*XXIII.59–110 is an important intertext here.

271　　visus . . . mihi – sc. *est*. This is the first point in his own narrative where Aeneas refers to himself directly. **largosque . . . fletus**: 'copious tears', a detail amplified by the abstract plural **fletus**.

272　　raptatus . . . ut quondam – sc. *erat*. This description of Hector's disfigurement is provided by Aeneas as narrator, unlike the dream-world exclamations at 274 and the ensuing dialogue. **aterque** – an epithet transferred from the blood (**cruento**) to **Hector**.

273　　traiectus lora – a participle phrase with retained accusative, **lora** (210n.): 'pierced *by* leather straps'. **tumentes** – the dead feet are pictured, vividly, still swelling.

274　　ei – with dative **mihi**, the exclamation to express immediate anguish: 'Woe upon me!', or a less archaic equivalent. **qualis erat** – the first of two exclamations. **qualis** is substantive: '*What sort of a man he was!*' **quantum mutatus**– sc. *et* after **erat** and *est* after **mutatus**. **quantum** is adverbial: 'how greatly'.

275　　redit – present tense retained for vividness to signify the abiding image of Hector as Troy's great 'returner', who in the *Iliad* memorably returns to the fighting in Book VI but fatally refuses to return home in Book XXII. He is a threshold character situated, literally and figuratively, between far-off fighting and domestic duty. **exuvias indutus Achilli** – another retained accusative (210n.): 'draped in the spoils of Achilles'. Patroclus in the *Iliad* dons Achilles' armour in order to boost Greek morale in his friend's absence. When he is killed, Hector takes the armour as a trophy.

276　　Danaum Phrygios – juxtaposed* to emphasize how matched the two armies once were. The Trojan assault on the beached

Greek ships (*Il.* XVI.112–29) was the closest they came to a decisive victory.

278   quae circum plurima muros / accepit – In *Iliad* XXIII, it is around the tomb of Patroclus that Achilles drags Hector's corpse.

280   voces – a poetic synonym for *verba*.

281   o lux Dardaniae – **o lux** and its chiastic* other half, **spes o**, are both terms of endearment which found their way into Roman comedy via Greek tragedy and Homer (e.g., *Il.*XVIII.102, where Achilles scolds himself for not being a 'saving light' (φάος) for Patroclus). Together with the vocative **exspectate 283** and the conversational **ille nihil, moratur 287**, Virgil conveys the familiarity of cousins.

282   quae tantae . . . morae – the first of two brief questions which carry the urgency of a mid-battle exchange. In his bewildered state, Aeneas is unaware that Hector has fallen, something the whole city well knew.

283   ut – to be taken with **aspicimus**, not **defessi 285**: 'How we see you . . .' The **post** phrases help to delay **aspicimus**, which is emphasized by enjambment* and the caesura which follows. **tuorum** – 'your kin'.

286   foedavit – 55n. This is the first, somewhat belated, perception of the wounds that the narrator Aeneas has already detailed. **vultus** – poetic plural.

287   ille nihil – sc. *respondit*. A conversational ellipsis (281n.). There is pathos in the contrast between Aeneas' intimate tone and Hector's terse commands. **nec me . . . moratur** – 'nor does he *heed* me . . .' – another colloquial usage of *moror* (cf. 102n.).

288   gemitus . . . ducens – 'drawing groans'. It is grim and effortful for Hector to describe his city's destruction, and the line's rhythm relays that: two caesurae in the second and fourth feet which rest the ear after **graviter** and **imo**, words which reinforce one another.

289   fuge – Aeneas in the *Iliou Persis*, a lost work of the Epic Cycle, flees the city after the death of Laocoon and before the symbolic execution of Priam – just as Hector counsels him here. Virgil needs Aeneas present at the king's death, for narratorial and thematic reasons. **nate dea** – vocative noun modified by an ablative of origin: '[you] goddess-born'. Aeneas' parentage makes Hector's instructions more plausible, more feasible and more binding. At this moment, Aeneas is elevated in stature above Hector: Homer's old champion must pass on to Aeneas (and to Virgil) responsibility for Troy. **his flammis** – 134n.

291   sat ... datum – sc. *est a te*. Like a front-line despatch, Hector's language in 290–1 is paratactic* and abrupt.

292   possent, defensa fuissent – If the city could be defended (at this time – imperfect **possent** for present time) it would have required Hector (pluperfect **fuissent** for an unfulfilled possibility). **defensa fuissent** – a metrically convenient alternative to *defensa essent*. **etiam hac** – 'by this [fighting] arm also'. Hector died before the Horse had entered, and so presumably he means more generally that, if the war was ever winnable, it was while he still lived.

293   sacra suosque ... penates – *penates* were 'pantry gods', an assortment of tutelary deities particular to a household, cupboard-sized and carrying family-specific significance. On a state level, the *penates* were those gods identified by the citizen body as long-standing patrons. **Troia** – Virgil's hero will be answerable first and foremost to his state, not his family or his own *gloria*.

294   hos ... his – an energetic line, to be delivered emphatically. The general density of demonstratives in Hector's speech (289, 292)

A
Level

conjures an image of him gesticulating vehemently. **moenia ...
magna** – i.e., Lavinium, where Aeneas will rule with his queen,
Lavinia. Rome itself will be founded generations later by Romulus
(I.254–96). **statues quae denique** – a decisive future indicative follows
the imperatives (**cape, quaere**). Take **quae** after **magna,** at the head of
its clause.

296   manibus – instrumental ablative with **effert 297.** When Aeneas
awakes, there is no sign of Hector's *penates.* It turns out to be Panthus,
a priest of Apollo, who has salvaged Troy's gods from the citadel (320).
Aeneas takes Panthus with him into the fray, presumably leaving the
icons at Anchises' house (321). The *penates* reappear next at 717, when
Aeneas tells his father to bring them as they flee. **Vestamque** – Vesta
could mean a garlanded effigy (**vittas**), a little like the Palladium, or
a portable hearth containing a sacred flame (297). Vesta (in Greek,
Hestia) was closely associated with Rome's own *penates*; Tacitus tells
us that a shrine of Vesta *cum penetralibus populi Romani* was lost in
the Great Fire of 64 AD (*Annals* XV.41).

297   aeternum ... ignem – the cult of Vesta was the responsibility
of Vestals, virgin priestesses who tended the sacred flame, a symbol of
Rome's permanence, within each temple. **adytis ... penetralibus** – an
ablative of separation with **effert.** It is unclear how we should visualize
the 'innermost chamber'.

298–317: Aeneas is jolted into action

Aeneas wakes and has a choice: should he stay or should he go? His
city is falling like trees flattened by floods (*praecipites* 307), but the
sight of his own neighbourhood in flames overwhelms him: *furor
iraque* flood him (*praecipitat* 317) and he chooses to die defending his
city.

**A
Level**

Deiphobus' extensive home (*ampla . . . domus* 310–11) is one of many references to Troy's former stature (cf. 56, 192, 290) and looks ahead to the pathos of Priam's upturned palace (483n.). See pp.6–7 for other elements of the *urbs capta* motif in *Aeneid* II.

298   diverso. . .luctu – 'distant lamentation' rather than 'lamentation everywhere'. **diverso** allows for both meanings, but this is a Virgilian hypallage,* transferring *diversus* from **moenia** to **luctu**. **miscentur** – meaning 'thrown into confusion': 'the walls *were beset* with distant lamentation'.

300   Anchisae – the first mention of Aeneas' father.

301   clarescunt – found only here in Virgil, and elsewhere used only of light, not sound. Its irregular application here suits the turmoil which confronts Aeneas' senses when he wakes. **armorumque ingruit horror** – 'the clashing of arms encroached'. *horror* has a physical sense here: 'a shaking, a shudder'. *ingruo* is similarly immediate: lit. 'I rush upon'.

302   excutior = *me excutio*: cf. the reflexive, quasi-Greek, use of the passive at 210 and 218. **somno** – ablative of separation. **fastigia** – poetic plural. This belongs to a dense clause in which **summi** and **ascensu** double-up their respective details, **fastigia** and **supero**. An elaborate lead-in to the alliteration* of **atque . . . asto** and Aeneas' first simile of the book.

304   veluti cum flamma – a two-headed simile comparing the Greeks' rampage first to fire and then to a flood (**torrens 305**). **furentibus Austris** – the *Auster*, a hot southerly wind, gets its name from the Sanskrit stem *ush-*, 'to burn'. **furentibus** compounds the hotness of the *Auster* and resonates thematically, at a moment when Aeneas' self-control will be tested. See 'Snakes and fire', pp.15–18.

A Level

305 **torrens** – derived originally from *torreo*, 'I scorch', and so subtly yoking **flamma 304** with **flumine**: fire and water and nature's destructive potential.

306 **sternit ... sternit** – huge, impersonal forces wreak indiscriminate damage, pausing not even for an *et* to join these clauses. **agros ... sata laeta boumque labores** – first the fields then their contents, detailed for additional pathos. In the personification* of **laeta**, and perhaps also **labores** ('exertions'), the simile* evokes the Trojan mood of the previous night and the relief they must have felt.

307 **praecipitesque ... silvas** – *praeceps* ('headlong') in verse, and especially in action narrative, expresses violent speed. **stupet inscius** – the delay of the subject, **pastor 308**, briefly isolates these words from the simile; we see the real Aeneas in alarm before we see the figurative shepherd. **inscius** – 'ignorant' in that the treachery of Sinon is not immediately obvious. Greeks are attacking Troy (the **horror** registered at 301), but to Aeneas their means of entry is disturbingly unclear.

309 **tum vero** – 105n. **manifesta fides** – sc. *est. fides* (here 'trustworthiness') has occurred twice in the book so far, both times – ironically – during the speech of Sinon (143, 161). Here Aeneas comprehends (as narrator and as actor) just how trustworthy the Greeks are: tragically *un*trustworthy.

310 **Deiphobi** – a son of Priam and Hecuba, a prominent hero in the *Iliad*, and one of the souls encountered by Aeneas in the Underworld (VI.494f.). **dedit ... ruinam** – a periphrastic expression for 'collapsed'. The first **iam** propels us into the detail of Deiphobus' house, but there's no time to dwell: with the second **iam** (311) we lurch to the next house, as if Aeneas' narrative is struggling to keep up with the spreading flames.

A Level

311 Volcano superante – Vulcan, the blacksmith god, is a common metonym* for fire. **domus** governs **dedit 310** but serves too as the implied object of **superante**. *supero* means both 'I overtop' and 'I overwhelm'. **proximus ardet / Ucalegon** – Ucalegon, a neighbour of Aeneas and Deiphobus, is a very minor character taken from the *Iliad* (III.148). As in the line above, Virgil elevates the pathos by specifying the individual in distress ('particularization'). Whether Ucalegon is actually alight, or whether his name stands for his house ('neighbouring Ucalegon̲'s̲'), is left grimly ambiguous; Ucalegon never resurfaces in the *Aeneid*.

312 Sigea ... freta – Sigeum is a promontory (modern Fort Kumkale) located eight kilometres north-west of Troy. **igni** – the ablative singular ending more common for *ignis* than -*e*.

313 exoritur – with this dactyl Virgil jolts us into the next stage in the narrative: the immediate threat to Aeneas himself. The ringing assonance* of **clamorque ... clangorque** anticipates the melee.

314 arma amens capio – a key line for Aeneas' (self-)characterization here, and for the poem's conception of heroic conduct. *amens* in Book II sticks close to its basic definition, 'bereft of good sense', and therefore 'reckless, impulsive, foolish'. Aeneas uses the word for Panthus, a grandfather and a priest (296n.), at 321, and for himself again at 745 in a moment of self-reproach. **nec sat rationis in armis** – sc. *est*. **sat**(is) **rationis** is a partitive genitive construction, lit. 'enough of rationale'.

315 bello – a dative of purpose (= *ad bellum*). **arcem** – 41n.

316 ardent animi – referring still only to Aeneas: 'my instincts yearned'. **mentem** – 'reasoning, thinking', here used equivalently to **rationis 314**.

317 praecipitat – 'rushes', even 'scrambles' (307n.). **pulchrumque
mori succurrit**– sc. *esse* and *mihi*: 'dying beautifully occurs to me'.
pulchrum qualifies the infinitive **mori**. Aeneas has only one solution:
arma, armis (314) and now **armis** again. The initial idea of **314 (arma
amens capio)** is enlarged in practical terms (**glomerare, concurrere**)
and then ethical terms (**pulchrum mori**).

*318–69: Aeneas and his Trojans begin their skirmish. The first Trojan he
encounters is Panthus, a priest of Apollo who has escaped the chaos with
his grandson. Panthus gives a pessimistic report of Greeks running
amok. Aeneas is again spurred to action. Others join him, including
Coroebus who is engaged to Cassandra, the priestess daughter of Priam.
Aeneas delivers some rousing words then leads his band into the fray
'like ravening wolves' (lupi ceu raptores 355–6).*

*Aeneas, in narrator mode, laments the death and destruction he
witnessed: the streets were littered with bodies – Greek as well as Trojan.*

370–558: Skirmishes, Pyrrhus and Priam

370–85: The death of Androgeos

Until this point, it is the Trojans who have suffered for their trusting
nature (see pp.13–15). Now it is the Trojans who turn to *fraus* and
dolus, and a Greek, Androgeos, is the unsuspecting victim.

370 primus se ... offert – 'Androgeos was the first to present
himself.' **Danaum** – applying to both **primus** and **caterva**, but translate
with the latter only.

371 Androgeos – a Greek with no known backstory. The final -*os*
syllable is long (Ἀνδρόγεως). Most editions, this included, Latinize
the genitive singular at 392, giving **Androgei** rather than *Androgeo*.
socia agmina credens – sc. *nos esse*. **agmina** is poetic plural.

**A
Level**

372   inscius – recalling **stupet inscius** (307n.). On this verbal cue, the poem reassigns the roles of deceiver and deceived.

374   ferunt – here meaning 'plunder, pillage'.

373   nam – a strengthening particle common in colloquial speech, especially in questions. The tone is more exhortatory ('Come now, what …?') than explanatory ('For what …?').

375   vos – to be taken in contrast with **alii 374** and implying an adversative particle like *sed* or *tamen*.

376   satis – modifying **fida:** 'sufficiently credible'.

377   sensit delapsus – imitating an 'accusative + participle' indirect statement, which Greek uses after verbs of perception. When the subject of the introductory verb (**sensit**) also governs the participle, it becomes a *nominative* + participle: hence the case of **delapsus**, qualifying Androgeos, the subject of **sensit**.

378   pedem … repressit – subverting the common idiom for retreat, *pedem refero*: Androgeos freezes, and checks himself mid-step. **pedem cum voce** – a zeugma,* dependent on **repressit**, which conveys the speed and totality of his reaction.

379   aspris – contracted form of *asperis*, for metrical convenience. The ablative case of **aspris … sentibus** denotes place where, with preposition *in* omitted. **veluti qui** – sc. *aliquis* before **qui**: 'as one who …'. Virgil evokes, and enlarges, the simile at *Iliad* III.33–5, where Paris retreats from Menelaus during their duel.

380   humi – locative, to be taken adverbially with **nitens**, 'treading hard *on* the ground'.

381   attollentem iras – a highly concentrated phrase which substitutes **iras** for more typical objects of *attollo* like *oculos* or *animos*. **caerula colla** – accusative of respect (cf. 57n.), because *tumeo* is intransitive. Translate as if **tumentem** is transitive: 'swelling its blue-green neck'.

382 haud secus – a typical formula for 'collecting' a simile and putting us back into the narrative. **visu tremefactus** – cf. **visu exsangues 212** and **tremefacta** 228, both describing the Trojans' horror as the snakes come for Laocoon. The verbal correspondence invites comparison between then and now, and inversion of the earlier predator–prey relationship. **abibat** – the imperfect is either conative, 'tried to withdraw', or inceptive, 'began to withdraw'.

383 circumfundimur – *nos circumfundimus*: a use of the passive voice equivalent to Greek's reflexive middle (302n.).

384 ignarosque loci – sc. *eos* as the object of **sternimus**, modified by both **ignaros** and **captos**.

386–434: Coroebus and Cassandra

The ploy of Coroebus to dress in Greek armour is a Virgilian invention which dramatizes the moral ambiguity of any armed conflict. Gordon Williams described the tone of Aeneas in these lines as 'almost a witness speaking before a jury in his own defence' (*Technique and Ideas in the* Aeneid, 252).

386 hic – temporal (122n.). **exsultans** – the sort of detail, in Book II, that never bodes well (cf. **gaudent 239** and **laeta 395**).

387 qua – an adverb ('where') formed from the abbreviation of *qua via*, 'by what route'. **salutis /. . . iter** – 'the path of survival', meaning more 'the way to fight back' than 'the way to escape'.

388 quaque ostendit se dextra – sc. *esse*: 'and where she [**Fortuna 387**] shows herself to be favourable'. **sequamur, mutemus, aptemus** – exhortative subjunctives: 'let us . . .'.

**A
Level**

390 dolus an virtus, quis … requirat? – *quis in hoste requirat utrum dolus an virtus sit?* The inverted word order and omission of *sit* and *utrum* (often omitted, even in prose) gives the sense of Coroebus' roused state. **requirat**, a potential subjunctive, introduces the indirect alternative question. **in hoste** – colloquial for 'when dealing with an enemy'.

391 ipsi – i.e., the Greeks killed in 384–5.

392 clipeique insigne decorum – the neuter noun **insigne** (less common than the adjective *insignis*) is governed by **induitur 393**, which functions like a Greek reflexive-middle (cf. 218, 511) with a direct object: 'puts on himself'. The natural direct object, the shield (**clipeique**) has become a subjective genitive dependent on **insigne**: 'the shield's blazon'.

394 ipse Dymas – **ipse** is here equivalent to *sua sponte* ('by his own initiative'), expressing the vigour of Dymas (and Rhipeus?).

396 haud numine nostro – sc. *ducente*: lit. 'with an unfamiliar divine power guiding'. The meaning is suitably ambiguous, because Aeneas the narrator is still computing what happened in the darkness – literal and metaphorical – of Troy's final night. He could simply mean that, disguised as Greeks, they fought under the auspices of anti-Trojan gods. Equally, the phrase could refer vaguely to the sense, recollected, of skirmishing in an alien emotional state.

397 per caecam … noctem – Aeneas personifies the night, but there is also a hint of narratorial hindsight in using an epithet more appropriate for his comrades – especially in light of **caecique furore 244. conserimus** – governing **proelia 397**, a Virgilian variation on *proelium committo*, 'I join battle'. **Orco** – dative expressing motion towards (= *ad Orcum*). Orcus was a god of the Underworld, known – poignantly, in the context of Book II – as the avenger of perjured oaths. *Orcus* here is a metonym,* standing for the Underworld generally.

398 diffugiunt – the *dis-* prefix sends the *-fugiunt* in different directions, suggesting a chaotic rout: a scene which must have consoled Aeneas to recall.

399 cursu – ablative of manner: 'at a run', i.e., as quickly as possible.

400 fida – qualifying **litora 399** and enjambed for prominence. The application of *fidus* to the Greek shoreline contributes to the problematic, or at least ambiguous, status of 'good faith' in this section, and in the book generally. **pars** – governing **scandunt 401** and completing the 'some . . . others . . .' construction begun with **diffigiunt alii 399. formidine turpi** – ablative of manner: 'in shameful terror'.

401 nota . . . in alvo – 'in its familiar belly'. This line, the book's final reference to the Horse, echoes the beginning of this section (237–8) by evoking the belly/womb metaphor (51, 238).

401 fas quemquam fidere – sc. *est*. See 157n. for the meaning of *fas*. **nihil** – adverbial: 'not at all'. This is a more emphatic version of *nefas est quemquam fidere quidquam divis invitis*, which gives a more strident tone to the narratorial comment.

402 ecce – 57n. **trahebatur** – the imperfect tense makes this brief shot of Cassandra 'move' effectively. **passis** – from *pando*, 'I spread out'. Here, with **crinibus**, as ablative of description: 'with hair dishevelled'. Horsfall (2008, p.322), 'The whole narrative breathes the immediacy of direct, oracular testimony.'

404 adytisque Minervae – The Greek rampage has no regard for the sanctity of Cassandra's refuge or her status: young and royal (**Priameia virgo 403**) but also a priestess, even if one serving Apollo not Minerva.

405 ardentia lumina . . ./ lumina – The repetition of **lumina**, an instance of epanalepsis,* enlarges their significance. It is a powerful picture painted by Virgil, especially when we set **ardentia** against the blackness of the night sky (cf. 397).

407 non tulit – 'he could not bear it'. These two words make us see both **hanc speciem** and the distressing sight of 404–6 through the eyes of Coroebus, a sort of retroactive focalization (see 'Narratorial standpoint', pp. 10–13). From the perspective of her fiancé, the pain and powerlessness of Cassandra is all the more intense. **furiata mente** – ablative of manner (cf. 314n.).

408 periturus – referring both to the outcome, known to our narrator, and Coroebus' unflinching fatalism: cf. Priam **moriturus 511**.

409 densis ... armis – ablative of description, rather than an indirect object of **incurrimus**.

410 primum – signposting the narrative (cf. *ecce*), and 'keeping time', along with **tum 413** and **etiam 420**, during a high-tempo action sequence. **delubri culmine** – i.e., the roof of Minerva's temple, where Coroebus has gone (404). The presence of other Trojans already fighting at the temple is unexplained and perhaps unimportant.

411 obruimur oriturque – The Trojans, now beset, lose their grip on the main verbs, first becoming passive subjects and then being dispossessed altogether by **caedes**.

412 facie ... errore – causal ablative. Take **errore** as 'confusion' rather than 'mistake', in order to suggest an ongoing state. **iubarum** – objective genitive dependent on **errore**, i.e., 'confusion of [= as to] the helmet crests'.

413 gemitu ... ereptae virginis ira – two ablatives of manner (**gemitu, ira**) effectively functioning as a hendiadys* ('with an angry cry'). **ereptae virginis** – another objective genitive, with **ira**. English might express this with a noun phrase: 'the girl's rescue'.

414   Aiax / et gemini Atridae – three Greeks of the highest profile (104n.). This Ajax is the 'Lesser', son of Oileus.

415   Dolopumque – The *Dolopes* hailed from Thessaly in northern Greece, the region home to Achilles and his son Pyrrhus (469ff.), who we can assume is commanding these Greeks.

416   adversi . . . venti – an image modelled on *Iliad* XVI.765–9, where the east and west winds rip through a wood. **rupto . . . turbine** – ablative absolute: 'when a storm has broken'. **ceu** – a common conjunction for starting similes (cf. 516). **quondam** – modifying both **rupto** and **confligunt 417** and here with an indefinite, generalizing sense: 'at some time or other'.

417   Zephyrusque Notusque – the west and south winds respectively. Notus (Νότος) was the Greek equivalent of Auster (305n.). **laetus Eois / Eurus equis**: 'the East wind, thrilling in the horses of Dawn'. A striking image which contrasts in tone with the grim intervention of Nereus (**saevitque 418**).

419   Nereus – the old man of the sea, a child of Gaia (the Earth) and Pontus (the sea); he is, usually, benevolent like his father. **imo . . . fundo** – ablative of place whence: Nereus churns the seas (**aequora**) 'from their deepest depths'.

420   si quos – after *si, nisi, num* and *ne* the pronoun *quis, quid* has an indefinite sense: 'if any', meaning 'whomsoever', with **illi** the antecedent, referring to the Greeks scattered in 396–401. **obscura nocte** – a phrase corresponding to **per caecam noctem 397** and signalling a return to the narrative's standpoint prior to the Cassandra episode.

421   totaque ... urbe – local ablative: 'throughout the city'. **insidiis**, however, is an instrument governed by **fudimus**.

422   primi – a confusing detail, given the Trojans are already under attack by Greeks (413–15). We infer that these Greeks are the 'first to recognize' *and explain* the Trojans' disguise. **mentitaque tela** – 'and the deceiving arms' (213n.).

423   ora sono discordia – lit. 'our mouths, jarring in their sound'. In Homer, Trojans and Greeks speak the same language, a convention which allows for dialogue between heroes on opposing sides. **sono discordia** could mean 'differing in the words sounded' or 'differing in the pronunciation of familiar words'. The latter is perhaps supported by **responsa ... fida <u>satis</u> 376–7**, which suggests Androgeos grasped most of the Trojan speech.

424   ilicet – an adverb which in Virgil dramatically prefaces peril or disaster: a blend of *heu, ecce* and adverbial *hic*. **obruimur** – Coroebus' rage was the catalyst for this action at 411; now the identical verb returns to claim the life of Coroebus, first, and then four comrades.

425   Penelei – Peneleus is mentioned in the *Iliad* (2.494) as a Boeotian commander. **divae armipotentis** – a grand, archaic* compound epithet. Minerva is unnamed, but clearly signified: the **aram** belongs to the temple where Cassandra was attacked (403–4).

426   unus – a colloquial usage which strengthens the superlative **iustissimus**: 'the most remarkably just man'. These adjectives belong to the relative clause in the line below.

427   in Teucris – 'among the Trojans'. **servantissimus aequi** – Virgil converts *servans*, originally a present participle, to an adjective governing an objective genitive, **aequi**: 'the most watchful of [i.e., concerned for] fairness'.

A Level

428   **dis aliter visum** – sc. *est*. **dis** is a contraction of dative *divis*. This stark comment on the fate of Rhipheus could belong, as a parenthesis, to either Aeneas or the poem's principal narratorial voice (the 'I' of *arma virumque cano*). **Hypanisque Dymasque** – Trojan fortunes unravel more quickly with the double *-que*, a linguistic bonding in death of the two companions.

429   **sociis** – further 'blue on blue' fatalities to compound the pathos of 410–12. **Panthu** – contrived from the Greek vocative form, Πάνθοε. Panthus is introduced at 318 as **arcis Phoebique sacerdos**. This is the first of Aeneas' two pathetic apostrophes.*

430   **pietas** – the predominant attribute which Aeneas strives for throughout the poem. The deaths of Panthus and Rhipheus, and Priam, exemplify that war, once raging, is blind to *pietas*. **infula** – a sacred woollen headband which indicated the wearer's religious consecration and inviolability: interchangeable with *vitta* (221n.).

431   **Iliaci cineres** – vocative but also the implied object of **testor** **432**. It is usually the gods or a *numen* (cf. 154–5) who are invoked by *testor*. **flamma extrema** – i.e., the city's funeral pyre.

432   **testor** – invoking the **cineres** and **flamma** of 431, but also introducing an indirect statement, with *me* as the implied accusative subject and **vitavisse** and **meruisse** as the infinitives. **ullas** – grammatically qualifying **vices 433** but understood with **tela** too.

433   **vices Danaum** – with **ullas 432**: 'any perils of [fighting off] the Greeks'. *vices* has the basic meaning 'changes'. Aeneas here refers to the hazardous flux of skirmishing. **Danaum** also goes with **tela 432. si fata fuissent** – 54n.

434   **ut caderem** – 'that I should fall': a noun clause functioning as the complement of **fata**. The imperfect subjunctive is determined by **si fuissent**, which puts **ut caderem** in virtual historic sequence.

**A
Level**

meruisse manu – '[I testify that I] earned [that I should fall] by my own hand'. **manu** - meaning vigorous involvement in battle.

434–52: Pyrrhus at the palace of Priam

The palace of Priam symbolizes the city's former prosperity and the harmony of its royal household. The degree of detail in Aeneas' narrative paints a lucid picture of what is lost and invests us deeply in what looms for the king of Troy.

The futility of Aeneas' intervention on the rooftop contrasts with the violent momentum of Pyrrhus as he breaches the palace entrance with all the destructive connotations of snakes and fire (see pp.15–18). The focalization through Pyrrhus at this moment effectively dispossesses Aeneas as the internal narrator, as if Virgil (or Pyrrhus?) has temporarily taken charge of the narrative.

434   divellimur inde – it is unclear exactly who or what 'wrenches' the Trojans from their present location.

435   Iphitas et Pelias – two Trojans not attested elsewhere, in this poem or the Epic Cycle at large.

436   iam gravior aevo – **aevo** is a causal ablative: 'by this point somewhat heavier [i.e., slower] due to his age'. **vulnere tardus Ulixi** – 'slowed down by a wound from Ulysses'. The genitive **Ulixi** is subjective: 'the wound *of* [i.e., inflicted by] Ulysses'.

437   protinus – with *ad*: 'straight to …'. **clamore vocati** – either 'summoned with a shout' (**clamore** instrumental ablative) or 'summoned because of a shout' (**clamore** causal ablative): either is possible.

438   ingentem pugnam – separated by some distance from its verb, **cernimus 441**, and so functioning like a headline. The initial three spondees allow our attention to linger before the hypothetical clause begins. The imperfect subjunctives (**forent, morerentur**), as with conditional clauses, refer to present time and actions which are now unfulfillable: 'as if there were [now] no other battles anywhere [but there are]'.

439 **forent** = *essent.* **tota . . . in urbe** – 'anywhere in the city'.

440 **sic** – collecting **ceu 438** and introducing its consequence: '[as if] ... and so'. **Martem** – a familiar metonym* in epic. Mars is the embodiment of unbridled bloodshed in battle. **tecta** –either the entire palace complex (*tectum* as 'building') or the rooftop (*tectum* as a roof covering). Both are possible, as we are coming into a section of 'split-screen' narrative, where the Greeks attack the entrance and the Trojans defend it from the palace roof.

441 **acta testudine** – ablative instrument with **obsessum**. A *testudo* ('tortoise') was both a shield-formation and a wheeled protective screen housing a battering ram. *agere* is the standard Latin verb for operating a ram.

442 **parietibus** – the first *-i-* is consonantal, which lengthens the first syllable. **postesque sub ipsos** – *sub* here meaning 'right beside, up against'.

443 **nituntur gradibus**: 'they strive up the rungs'. The subject of the main verb becomes, implicitly, the Greeks: a subtle shift as Greek ascendancy becomes more pronounced. **ad tela** – 'to' with a sense of 'against'.

444 **protecti** – the perfect-ness of this participle sounds awkward with the present tense **obiciunt**, when rendered literally: 'having been protected, they hold out [their shields]'. The solution is to turn **protecti** into a predicative noun: 'as protection'.

A Level

445   contra – adverbial, marking a dramatic transition in the action narrative. **turres … domorum / 446 culmina** – both **turres** and **culmina** belong to **domorum**. *turris* is less 'tower' and more 'battlement' here. *culmina* could also mean no more than 'roof tiles' pulled up as makeshift missiles.

446   his – an instance of hyperbaton* (along with **se … defendere**): **his** qualifies **telis 447**, and the promotion of **his** makes the demonstrative doubly emphatic. **quando ultima cernunt** – sc. *adesse*: 'when they see that the end is near'. This is the relative, rather than interrogative, *quando*. **ultima** (lit. 'final things') is ambiguous until **extrema … in morte** in the line below.

447   extrema iam in morte – an epic periphrasis for *iam morituri*. They are not yet dying, as *in* + ablative might imply, but they are undoubtedly doomed – at least from the retrospective viewpoint of Aeneas.

448   decora alta – metaphorically 'high', meaning rare and exquisite.

449   alii – i.e., the other Trojans stationed to resist those Greeks ramming the palace entrance (440–1). **imas** – 'below', distinguishing the two zones of activity: the roof and the front steps of the palace.

450   obsedere – the action belonging here to the defenders (**alii**), rather than the attackers (**obsessumque 441**). The pressure builds on either side of the critical entry point. Translate *obsideo* here as 'take up position'.

451   instaurati – sc. *sunt*. This expression, equivalent to a verb of desiring (e.g., *cupiebam*) accounts for the three infinitives which follow. **animi** – poetic plural.

452   vimque addere victis – Aeneas' determination rings rhetorically through the alliteration,* the choice of **victis**, and the whole-line chiasmus.*

453 caecae – as in a road's 'blind corner'. The door is recessed somehow and therefore not visible from the palace's exterior. **pervius usus / 454 tectorum inter se** – lit. 'a feature of the palace giving access within itself'. **pervius usus** – equivalent to *via utilis*, but emphasizing the usefulness of the passageway rather than the passageway itself.

455 a tergo – with **postesque 454**, as if an adjective: 'rear door'. **qua** – 387n.

456 Andromache – the wife of Hector and mother of their infant son, Astyanax. Andromache and Astyanax in the *Iliad* (VI.388f.) are notoriously ill-fated: Astyanax will be thrown from the city ramparts and his mother will be enslaved.

457 avo – dative expressing motion towards (= *ad avum*). This variation, after **ad soceros**, is a metrical workaround. **Astyanacta** – Greek accusative. **trahebat** – habitual imperfect: 'used to take along'.

458 evado – Aeneas' private entryway has delivered him nearer the action at the front of the palace. He needs to 'get away' from this before he is embroiled and unable to reach the roof. The first-person of **evado** clarifies that Aeneas is now definitely alone. The elision of **evado ad** hastens his ascent, as if we hear him taking two steps at a time.

459 manu – adverbial, 'with vigour', rather than instrumental, 'by hand' (cf. 434).

460 turrim – 224n. **in praecipiti** – 'at the edge'. *praeceps*, with the meaning 'steeply descending', is used substantively here to mean 'a sheer drop': the **turrim** is built flush against the outer palace wall. **sub astra / 461 eductam** – lit. 'constructed up towards the stars': more naturally, 'rising up to the stars'.

461 tectis – ablative of separation: 'from the [top of the] palace roof'.

A Level

462   Danaum ... Achaica – both meaning 'Greek' (44n.). **solitae** – sc. *sunt* or *erant*, governing **videri 461**. The verb has three subjects (**Troia, naves, castra**), although the gender and number of **solitae** is determined by the nearest one, **naves**.

463   adgressi ferro – a participle phrase governing **turrim 460**. *ferrum* can serve for any metal implement: here in the plural most naturally translated as 'tools'. The sequence of five spondees in this line suits the heavy exertion of the Trojans. **circum** – adverbial: 'round all its sides'. **qua** – 387n. **labantes / 464 iuncturas** – lit. 'the slipping [i.e., separating] joints' of the tower.

464   iuncturas tabulata dabant – *do* meaning here 'offer, yield'. The sense seems to be that the tower's high stories (**summa ... tabulata**) make it less stable and more vulnerable to demolition.

465   altis/ 465 sedibus – 'from its high position': ablative of separation with **convellimus**, referring to the tower's elevation, set high on the palace roof. **ea** – i.e., the tower, converted here from object (**turrim 460**) to subject. **impulimusque** – a perfect amid a slew of presents: the so-called 'instantaneous' usage, marking a sudden and critical moment within a passage of continuous action.

467   ast – archaic *at*. **alii** – i.e., more Greeks trying to capture the rooftop. **incidit** – the decisive culmination of the previous seven lines.

468   telorum interea cessat genus – an unfinished line (66n.).

469   Pyrrhus – the 'flame-haired' (Greek πύρρος) son of Achilles, first mentioned at 263 by his alternative name, **Pelidesque Neoptolemus**: 'Neoptolemus, grandson of Peleus'. πύρρος is also used in Greek for bloodshot eyes, a subtle connection to the snakes' description at 210.

470   telis et luce coruscus aena – the hendiadys,* separating the weapons (**telis**) and their bronze lustre (**luce ... aena**), sharpens the image of Pyrrhus ablaze. The image is complex but it successfully evokes not just the glinting weapons but also the city's flaming backdrop and the snake's glistening back (**lubrica . . . terga 474**).

471   qualis ubi ... coluber – sc. *talis erat* to complete the correlative construction (cf. 223n.): lit. 'He was of such a kind as a kind of snake when ...'. Start a new sentence at 471: 'He was like a snake when ...'. **mala gramina**: 'poisonous herbs', the implied cause of the snake's swelling (**tumidum 472**) as well as its source of venom. **in lucem** describes the actions of line 474, **convolvit** and **sublato**.

472   quem – the pronoun which begins the relative clause of **472**: take before **frigida**.

473   positis. . .exuviis – 'with his skin sloughed'. **nitidusque iuventa** – lit. 'gleaming by [= in] his youthfulness'. **iuventa** is an ablative of respect.

475   linguis micat ore trisulcis – 'it flickers from its mouth with its triple-forked tongue'. **ore** is a local ablative, whereas **linguis** is instrumental. The plural, **linguis**, is used often for body parts but it also amplifies the image here. Snakes' tongues are forked as part of a complex olfactory system which helps them detect prey. Alongside this predatory connotation is the common usage of *mico* and *trisulcus* – and *coruscus* – to describe lightning strikes. **ad solem** reiterates **in lucem 471**, almost as epanalepsis.*

476   Periphas – the name of a Greek killed by Ares (Mars) in the *Iliad* (V.842f.). His epithet (πελώριος, 'awe-inspiring') resembles *ingens*, but clearly Virgil can revive only the name, not the man.

477   Automedon – the trusted charioteer of Achilles in the *Iliad* (e.g., XXIV.574f.). **Scyria pubes** – Scyros was the island ruled by Lycomedes, whose daughter Deidameia was the mother of Pyrrhus.

A
Level

Pyrrhus was summoned from Scyros by Odysseus in the later stages of the Trojan campaign (*Od*.XI.509).

479   ipse – i.e., Pyrrhus.

480   postesque a cardine vellit – a remarkable undertaking, trying to dismantle the fortified (**aeratos**) pivoting post (**postesque**) of each door from its socket (**cardine**). Given that Pyrrhus soon resorts to hacking through the door's panels, we should understand this initial **vellit** with a conative ('tried to . . .') or continuous ('kept on . . .') sense, as if the historic present were an imperfect.

481   cavavit – a shift to the perfect tense, signifying that the decisive breach has happened: this is now the beginning of the end for Priam.

482   robora – poetic plural. **ingentem . . . fenestram** – the concentric word order imitates the concentric hole Pyrrhus has created. A passage of heavy enjambment* culminates in **fenestram**, the first breach of the palace's defence, and a glimpse into the fraught interior for both Pyrrhus and the audience whose attention, for the last fourteen lines, has been glued to him. As we witness the scene inside the palace, we are looking through this 'window' and through the eyes of Pyrrhus.

483   apparet – the household 'becomes visible' to Pyrrhus. The narrative standpoint is wholly aligned with Pyrrhus for the next eight lines: Aeneas is still on the rooftop, with a very different perspective, and to him the palace interior is not a new sight (453–8). **patescunt** – more than a synonym for **apparet**, *patesco* suggests a steadily extending field of vision. The palace is so enormous that it takes a moment for Pyrrhus' eyes to survey the interior.

484   Priami – the first mention of Troy's king since 454. Priam and his residence symbolize the city's venerable status (cf. 56, 191, 437). The palace is identified by its owner so consistently that *Priami* functions almost as an epithet, and in this scene the poem exploits that association effectively: the countdown to Priam's death starts with the first breach of his palace's entrance, and the invasive gaze of Pyrrhus is the next wound struck.

485   videt – Pyrrhus, unexpressed, regains control of the main verbs. Although subtle, the shift is unambiguous because the interior scene is so strongly focalized. **in limine primo** – an echo of **primoque in limine 469**, although here referring to the area on the palace side of the door.

486   at – with this word, the narrative abandons the impending clash at the entrance and directs our gaze instead to the mournful interior.

487   miscetur – used abstractly to express confusion (298n.): 'the palace interior *is engulfed* by . . .'.

488   ululant – the symbolic significance of Priam's palace (484n.) invests the personification* of **aedes 487** with extra meaning. **ferit aurea sidera clamor** – capping an effective tricolon* of images (486–7), each of which characterizes the palace interior through sounds.

490   amplexaeque – with a present sense (213n.). **oscula figunt** – a very Roman gesture, conventional when leaving for the last time a familiar or cherished abode.

491   vi patria – 'with his father's ferocity'. This detail begins the implicit comparison between hero-types: Pyrrhus compared to Achilles, and also to Aeneas. **ariete crebro** – 'by constant ramming', with a causal sense. **ariete** is trisyllabic, with the *-i-* made consonantal in order to fit hexameters. *aries* could be a literal battering ram or a metonym* for 'battering blows'.

493   cardine – ablative of separation, with the singular noun serving both doorposts: 'from their sockets'.

A Level

494   **fit via vi** – an iconic *sententia*: terse, alliterative* and quotable.
primosque – substantive: 'the first men', i.e., the **armatosque ...
stantes** of 485. **trudicant** – a strong verb, applied originally to the
butchering of animals.

495   **loca** – *locum* in the plural: 'places, a district'. The masculine
locus means 'place' in the singular but in the plural 'passages in a text
or author'. **milite** – concrete for collective (= *militibus*).

496   **non sic** – with **fertur 498**: 'not so does [the river] rush', i.e., the
breaching of the entrance is *even worse* than when a river bursts its
banks. **aggeribus ruptis** – ablative motion whence, with **exiit 496**,
'[from] its burst banks'. **cum ... / 497 exiit ... evicit** – an indefinite
cum clause using the indicative: 'whenever ...'. This kind of *cum* clause
uses a tense 'one back' in time from the main clause tense. Here, the
main clause verbs are present (**fertur, trahit**), which determines the
perfects (**exiit, evicit**) in the *cum* clause.

497   **oppositasque ... moles** – lit. 'its opposing structures': more
naturally, 'its retaining banks'.

498   **cumulo** – ablative of manner, 'in a cresting wave', with **fertur**,
'rushes'. *feror* implies chaotic, surging movement (337, 511n.)

499   **vidi ipse** – with these emphatic words (amplified at 501),
Aeneas resurfaces for the first time since 465 as Dido's eyewitness
narrator. It is unclear how exactly Aeneas was witness to these events,
given he is still on the roof. **furentem / 500 caede** – ablative of manner,
'rampant in his slaughter', which echoes with variation a similar detail
in the simile, **furens cumulo 498**.

501   **vidi Hecubam centumque nurus** – Priam and his wife Hecuba
had fifty sons, each married, and fifty daughters (although only twelve
in the *Iliad*, VI.247f.). The **quinquaginta illi thalami** belong to the
sons, with each daughter living elsewhere with their husband,

under normal circumstances. *nurus* here includes both biological daughters and daughters-in-law. The repetition of *vidi* (**vidi 199**) makes an ominous connection between Priam and Pyrrhus, as objects of the same viewer and the same verb. **per** – expressing spatial extent, as most commonly, but here more 'among' than 'through'. The sense is of Priam's family filling the altar court. There is also the metrical utility of *per* being one syllable shorter than *apud*. **per aras** functions as the pivot between the palace pillaging and the death of Priam.

502   **quos ipse sacraverat ignes** – take **ignes**, the object of **foedantem** (55n.), before its relative pronoun **quos**.

504   **postes** – the doors of the inner chambers, easily confusable with the entrance doors of 480, 485 and 493. The **postes** of 490 clearly belong to the interior, as here. The doors at 504 are almost personified* in their grandeur through **superbi**. That adjective is qualified by two ablatives of description: **barbarico ... auro** ('oriental gold') and **spoliisque** ('trophies').

505   **procubuere** = *procubuerunt*. **qua deficit ignis** – 'where the fire is not'. For the adverbial *qua*, see 387n.

506–58: The deaths of Polites and Priam

The death of Polites is a pathetic precursor to the death of Priam, the climax of the book's middle section (see p.14). Priam is defined in this scene by his unfitness for epic: he is not a king but an old man now (*senior* 509), and the recurrence of *nequiquam* (510, 515, 546) marks the tragic irony* in his resistance.

Priam's intervention after the death of his son imitates a Homeric sequence whereby a hero throws insults, sometimes with a divine invocation, before throwing his spear. His last-ditch appeal to the

A
Level

gods, however, only confirms that *pietas* (536) is a concern for the human realm alone (see p.12).

506 requiras – potential subjunctive, qualified by **forsitan** and introducing the indirect question *quae fata Priami fuerint.* **et** is more adverbial here: 'perhaps you may *also* ask'. This address to Dido, the implied subject of **requiras**, casts Aeneas yet further in the role of impersonal messenger and less as the action protagonist we left behind at 468.

508 medium . . . hostem – the adjective here more naturally belongs to **penetralibus** ('the enemy, in the middle of the innermost quarters'). A kind of emphatic hendiadys* is achieved by the transfer of **medium**: the enemy is 'deep-deployed' and so now visible to Priam 'in the depths' of his home. The palace is stripped first of its adjectives, then of its king.

510 umeris – indirect object of **circumdat**. Shoulders are often mentioned in epic arming scenes (e.g., *Il.* XVI.40f. in which Patroclus takes Achilles' armour); here, they suggest the **arma** is either a shield or a breastplate.

511 cingitur – with a reflexive sense, using the passive voice like a Greek middle (393n.): 'he buckled on himself [his sword]'. **fertur** – 498n. **moriturus** – can carry a sense of purpose, '[as one intending] to meet death', as well as concession, 'though about to die'.

513 ingens ara fuit – This altar becomes the shrine of the Penates, a more domestically intimate Roman equivalent. The altarside is an ominous location by this point in Book II: Coroebus dies at the altar of Minerva less than 100 lines earlier (424–5), and the deaths of Sinon (foiled, 128–9) and Laocoon (figured, 223–4) happen at altar sites.

514 complexa – with a continuous sense, as also **amplexae 517** (213n.).

515   **altaria** – found always in the more metrically wieldy plural, in classical Latin. As at 550, translate as singular. **nequiquam** – describing **sedebant 517**.

516   **ceu ... columbae** – a short, taut simile which evokes *Il.* 22.138–42, and the pursuit of Hector by Achilles. At the death of Priam, we are visited, for a second time, by the ghost of Hector. On this, it is worth reading Angus Bowie's article 'The Death of Priam: allegory and history in the Aeneid', *Classical Quarterly* 40 (1990): 470–81. Achilles treated Hector's body brutally, but Priam in *Il.* 24 succeeds in stirring his opponent's empathy by evoking those human values which his son Pyrrhus will emphatically reject (547–50).

518   **sumptis . . . iuvenalibus armis** – ablative absolute.

519   **ut vidit** – with Hecuba the subject. **quae mens tam dira** – the primary meaning of *dirus* is 'ill-omened, portentous': here, 'what purpose so ill-conceived ...?'. Her criticism is offset by the pity in **miserrime coniunx**.

520   **his cingi telis** – translate as if *his te cingere telis* (511n.). **aut** – the colloquial usage found also at 43, 70, 127 and 286. The spoken idiom adds to the intimacy of their wavelength, putting more pathos into their interaction – which we sense could be their last.

521   **auxilio nec defensoribus** – the indirect objects of **eget 522**, which takes an ablative (of separation). **defensoribus** as 'defenders' sounds odd in reference to her husband's solo sally, but it refers in fact to **his . . . telis 520**. The predicament (**tempus 522**) requires neither his help nor his clunky old armour.

522   **si ipse meus . . . Hector** – 516n. The conditional construction is lacking its main clause, something like *tempus te egeret*: 'Not [even] if my Hector himself were now here *would the situation need you*', i.e., death and disaster is now unstoppable. **adforet** = *adesset*.

A Level

523   tandem concede – a tenderly pleading instruction which conveys well their domestic intimacy. **tandem**, like **aut 520**, derives from spoken idiom and carries the tone of 'Please dear, come here, really <u>no more</u> now.'

524   moriere – the contracted form of the future passive indicative second singular of mixed conjugation verbs (*morieris*). **sic ore effata** – a formula found in Ennius, which dignifies Hecuba's appeal and supplies a metrically useful disyllable, **ore**.

526   Pyrrhi – subjective genitive, denoting the source of the **caede**: 'the slaughter of [i.e., perpetrated by] Pyrrhus'. **Polites** – a minor son of Priam, mentioned at *Il.* II.791f. The elision of **ecce autem elapsus** is one of six instances in this section of seven lines.

528   porticibus longis – an ablative of extension: 'through(out) the long colonnades'.

529   saucius – postponed and run on for dramatic impact. **illum** – i.e., Polites. **ardens** – an appropriate epithet for the 'flame-haired' assailant (469n.). **infesto vulnere** – lit. 'with a danger-laden wound', meaning 'with a wound ready to inflict'. Polites is already wounded; Pyrrhus is now going for the killer blow.

530   iam iamque – 'now, now even', to be read with the breathless exertion of a sports commentator. **manu tenet** – 'grasps [him] with his hand'. A touch tautologous perhaps, but a phrase which anticipates the sharp detailing of Priam's death (**laeva dextraque 552**).

531   ante oculos . . . ora parentum – belonging to the **ut** temporal clause but more naturally translated with the delayed **concidit 532**.

533   in media . . . morte – lit. 'in the middle of death': a striking detail, given that Priam is yet unwounded. A more natural translation might be 'in death's very grip', as this captures the fatal predicament instead of the actual death throes.

534 **voci iraeque** – indirect objects of **pepercit**. The hendiadys* gives greater emphasis to **iraeque** than *voci iratae* could have achieved.

535 **at** – directing the tone, rather than content, of Priam's utterance. This use of *at* has a coercive force and occurs commonly in curses which confront, as here, an addressee. **at 540** is the regular adversative usage, 'but'. **pro talibus ausis** – 'in return for such brazen behaviour'. *ausum*, lit. 'thing done daringly', is a noun coined by Virgil from the perfect active participle of *audeo*, with the participle's voice becoming passive.

536 **di** = *dei*. **si qua est caelo pietas**: 'if there is any *pietas* up above'. **caelo** is a local ablative. The sense of *pietas* here is 'acknowledgment of a life lived dutifully'. Perhaps 'pity' best serves the context. **curet** – subjunctive to express either a generic idea ('if there is any *pietas* up there, of the sort which might intervene') or a purpose idea ('if there is any *pietas* up there, for the purpose of intervening').

537 **persolvant, reddant** – jussive subjunctives. Their indirect object, **tibi 535**, has been elevated to the top of the imprecation.

538 **qui** – antecedent **tibi 535**. This can be translated as a causal relative clause, as if **qui** were *quod*. In classical prose, the verb (**fecisti 539**) would be in the subjunctive to convey the imputed nature of the causal clause. The indicative, as here, belongs to colloquial Latin and gives Priam's words a certain directness.

539 **patrios . . . vultus**: a lofty alternative for *patris vultus*. **foedasti** = *foedavisti* (55n.).

540 **at non ille . . . Achilles / 541 talis** – 'But not at all was he, Achilles, like this . . .' **satum quo te mentiris** – take the relative pronoun at the clause's front, as usual. Supply *esse* to complete the indirect statement after **mentiris**.

541 **in hoste ... Priamo** – 'with Priam his enemy'. This use of *in*, meaning 'in the case of ...' or 'as regards ...', is only used to articulate human relationships (cf. 390n.). **iura fidemque / 542 supplicis** – *iura* are the rights a suppliant can expect; *fides* is the expectation of those rights.

542 **erubuit** – here taking a direct object: **iura fidemque 541**. **sepulcro** – indirect object of **reddidit 543**. The ransoming of Hector's corpse (*Il.* XXIV.468f.) is one of the most memorable scenes in Greek literature. Readers of the *Iliad*, though, may find Priam's recollection of Achilles' magnanimity somewhat selective.

544 **fatus** – sc. *est*; likewise for **repulsum 545**.

545 **rauco ... aero** – ablative instrument with **repulsum**.

546 **summo ... umbone** – local ablative denoting where the spear dangles from. *summus* here means 'the surface of' rather than 'the top of' the shield's boss.

547 **cui Pyrrhus** – sc. *dixit*. As curt as could be, especially by comparison to Priam's two-line equivalent (533–4).

548 **Pelidae genitori** – picking up Priam's invocation of Achilles (540) and using his opponent's words against him, as bullies do. The elevated register of a patronymic **Pelidae** (dative singular) with the grand **genitori** has a sarcastic edge to it.

549 **degeneremque Neoptolemum** – adjective used predicatively, rather than complementing an indirect statement with *esse* understood: 'Remember to tell him all about [**illi ... narrare memento**] my sorry behaviour **and his Neoptolemus, a reprobate**.' **memento** – a future imperative form with a present sense: the only imperative form of *memini*.

550 **morere** – another cold command, this time echoing Achilles' single word to Hector at *Il.* XXII.365 (τέθναθι). **altaria ad ipsa** –

suppliant is to become sacrifice (513n.). **trementem** – sc. *Priamum*. It is unclear whether the king trembles through fear or age. Servius favours the latter and the earlier **trementibus ... umeris 509–10** implies this is a characteristic tremor.

551   **in multo ... sanguine** – cf. **multo cum sanguine 532**. **lapsantem** – a gruesome, and rare, frequentative form of *labor*: 'slithering'.

552   **laeva dextraque** – two instrumental ablatives. The first of these actions suggests Pyrrhus intends to behead Priam, but it's the king's side where the sword enters first. We know from **avulsumque umeris caput 558** that Priam is later beheaded. **coruscum** – 'flashing', promoted for prominence (cf. 470).

553   **lateri** – a more metrically viable alternative for *in latus*. **capulo tenus** – the normal construction: *tenus* follows the ablative it governs.

554   **haec finis Priami fatorum** – sc. *erat*. Aeneas begins his epilogue (or epitaph?) with a response to 506, a piece of ring-composition typical of the poem. The formulation **haec finis**, as well as **hic exitus**, has historiographical analogues in both Latin and Greek, and evokes Plutarch's description of Pompey's shoreside death in 48 BC (see p.7). **illum** – governed by **tulit 555** and modified by **videntem 555**, **superbum 556** and (in apposition) **regnatorem 557**.

555   **sorte** – 'according to fate's decree', rather than 'by lot'. **hic exitus 554 ... sorte** functions therefore as a reiteration of **haec ... fatorum**. The historical and symbolic significance could not be stronger in these lines.

556   **populis terrisque** – causal ablative with **superbum**: 'proud in [= as a result of] his subject peoples and his territories'.

557   **ingens ... truncus** – Servius comments that this line 'touches on the story of Pompey' and Bowie (1990), cited at 516, suggests that

ingens here could allude to his cognomen, *Magnus*. **litore** – local ablative, 'on the shore'. Servius records an alternative version of Priam's death, carried out at the tomb of Achilles on the Troad coast. The desolate beachhead is an appropriately pathetic setting for Virgil to relocate the headless corpse of Priam, irrespective of the link to Pompey.

558   umeris – ablative of separation: 'from his shoulders'.

Vocabulary

An asterisk * denotes a word in OCR's Defined Vocabulary List for AS.

*a, ab + *abl.*	from, away from
abdo, abdidere, abdidi, abditum	I hide, bury
*abeo, abire, abii/ivi	I go away, withdraw
abstineo, abstinere, abstinui, abstentum	I hold back, refrain
accingo, accingere, accinxi, accinctum	I apply myself (235n.)
*accipio, accipere, accepi, acceptum	I receive; I hear (65)
accommodo, accommodare, accommodavi, accommodatum	I make fit; I attach (393)
*acer, acris, acre	sharp; fierce
acernus -a -um	maple
Achaicus -a -um	of Achaea (= Greek)
Achilles -is/ -i *m.*	Achilles (109n.)
Achivi -orum *m. pl.*	the Achaeans (= Greeks)
*ad + *acc.*	to, towards; at (202), near
*addo, addere, addidi, additum	I add, contribute
adfligo, adfligere, adflixi, adflictum	I afflict
*adgredior, adgredi, adgressus sum	I venture; I attack
*adhuc (*adv.*)	still

aditus -us *m.*	entrance
adsentio, adsentire, adsensi, adsensum	I approve (131)
adspiro, adspirare, adspiravi, adspiratum + *dat.*	I blow upon; I favour (385)
***adsum, adesse, adfui**	I am present
adversus -a -um	opposing
adytum -i *n.*	shrine, sanctuary
aedes, aedium *f. pl.*	residence
aeger, aegra, aegrum	sick; worn out (268)
aenus -a -um	bronze
aequor, aequoris *n.*	plain (69); sea (176)
aequum -i *n.*	fairness (427n.)
aeratus -a -um	bronze
aes, aeris *n.*	bronze
aeternus -a -um	everlasting
aether, aetheris *m.*	upper air, sky
aevum -i *n.*	age
agger, aggeris *m.*	mound, levee (496)
agitator, agitatoris *m.*	driver
agito, agitare, agitavi, agitatum	I drive off, harry
***agmen, agminis** *n.*	crowd (68); advancing enemy (212); massed troops (371, 466)
agnosco, agnoscere, agnovi, agnotum	I recognize
***ago, agere, egi, actum**	I conduct; I drive, compel; I form up (441)
Aiax, Aiacis *m.*	Ajax (414n.)
aio, ais, ait (*defect.*)	I say
aliqui, aliqua, aliquod	some, any (*indefinite adj.*)
***aliquis, aliquid**	someone, something (*pron.*); some ... (*adj.*)

aliter (*adv.*)	otherwise
*****alius, alia, aliud**	another, other
altaria, altarium *n.*	altar
*****altus -a -um**	high, tall; deep
altum -i *n.*	sea (203)
alvus, i *f.*	belly
ambiguus -a -um	doubtful; arousing suspicion
amens (*gen.* **amentis**)	mindless
amicus -a -um	warm, friendly
*****amicus -i** *m.*	friend
*****amitto, amittere, amisi,**	I lose
amissum	
amnis, amnis *m.*	river
amplector, amplecti, amplexus	I embrace
sum	
amplus -a -um	full; extensive (310)
Anchises -ae *m.*	Anchises (300n.)
Androgeos, -ei *m.*	Androgeos (371n.)
Andromache, Andromaches *f.*	Andromache (456n.)
anguis, anguis *c.*	snake
anima -ae *f.*	life, breath
*****animus -i** *m.*	heart, spirit (72, 120, 316); courage (61, 386, 451); soul (144)
*****annus -i** *m.*	year
*****ante** + *acc.*	before
antiquus -a -um	ancient (188); dear old (129)
*****aperio, aperire, aperui,**	I open up; I reveal (246)
apertum	
Apollo, Apollinis *m.*	Apollo
*****appareo, apparere, apparui,**	I appear
apparitum	

**apud + *acc.*	among
*ara -ae f.	altar
*arbor, arboris f.	tree
arceo, arcere, arcui	I restrain, confine
ardeo, ardere, arsi, arsum	I blaze, burn; rage; I yearn (105)
arduus -a -um	high
Argi -orum *m. pl.*	the city Argos (95, 179nn.)
Argivus -a -um	of Argos (= Greek)
Argolicus -a -um	of Argos (= Greek)
aries, arietis *m.*	battering-ram; ramming
*arma, armorum n.	weapons, armour
armentum -i *n.*	herd, flock
armiger, armigeri *m.*	arms-bearer
armipotens (*gen.* armipotentis)	strong-in-arms
arrigo, arrigere, arrexi, arrectum	I raise; I make alert, awaken (173n.)
*ars, artis f.	skill, craft, cunning
artifex, artificis *m.*	schemer (125)
artus -a -um	narrow, tight
artus -us *m.*	limb
arvum -i *n.*	field
arx, arcis f.	citadel
*ascendo, ascendere, ascendi, ascensum	I climb
ascensus -us *m.*	climb
Asia -ae f.	Asia Minor
asper, aspera, asperum	harsh, cruel
aspicio, aspicere, aspexi, aspectum	I behold
ast	but
asto, astare, asteti, astatum	I stand
astrum -i *n.*	star

Astyanax, Astyanactis *m.*	Astyanax (456n.)
ater, atra, atrum	dark, black
***atque**	and
Atridae -arum *m. pl.*	the sons of Atreus (104n.)
atrium -i *n.*	internal court
attollo, attollere	I raise up
auctor, auctoris *m.*	deviser (150)
***audeo, audere, ausus sum**	I dare
***audio, audire, audivi, auditum**	I hear, listen
aura -ae *f.*	air, breeze
auratus -a -um	golden
aureus -a -um	golden
auris, auris *f.*	ear
aurum -i *n.*	gold
Auster, Austri *m.*	the southerly wind (110, 304n.)
ausum -i *m.*	something dared
***aut**	or; and (45n.)
***autem**	however, but
Automedon, Automedontis *m.*	Automedon (477n.)
***auxilium -i** *n.*	help, support
aveho, avehere, avexi, avectum	I carry off; (*pass.*) I depart, sail away
avello, avellere, avulsi, avulsum	I steal away
aversus -a -um	hostile, opposed
avus -i *m.*	grandfather
axis, axis *m.*	heavens
barba -ae *f.*	beard
barbaricus -a -um	eastern, Oriental
Belides, Belidae *m.*	Palamedes (82n.)
***bellum -i** *n.*	war
bigae -arum *f. pl.*	two-horse chariot

bipennis, bipennis *f.*	double-headed axe
***bis**	twice
bos, bovis *c.*	ox, cow
bruma -ae *f.*	winter
***cado, cadere, cecidi, casum**	I fall
caecus -a -um	blind; dark, undetectable
caedo, caedere, cecidi, caesum	I kill, slaughter
***caelum -i** *n.*	sky, the heavens
caerulus -a -um	blue-green
Calchas, Calchantis *m.*	Calchas (100n.)
***campus -i** *m.*	plain, field
***cano, canere, cecini, cantum**	I sing; I predict (124)
***capio, capere, cepi, captum**	I take, capture
capulus -i *m.*	hilt
***caput, capitis** *n.*	head
cardo, cardinis *m.*	hinge; door socket (480, 493)
careo, carere, carui, **caritum** + *abl.*	be without, lack
carina -ae *f.*	keel; ship (198)
Cassandra -ae *f.*	Cassandra (246n.)
cassus -a -um + *abl.*	deprived of
casus -us *m.*	outcome; calamity
caterva -ae *f.*	crowd
***causa -ae** *f.*	cause, reason
caverna -ae *f.*	cavity, hollow (53)
cavo, cavare, cavavi, cavatum	I hollow out
cavus -a -um	hollow, empty
celsus -a -um	tall
centum (*indecl.*)	one hundred
***cerno, cernere, crevi, cretum**	I perceive, discern
certo, certare, certavi, certatum	I compete, strive

*certus -a -um	certain
cervix, cervicis *f.*	neck
cesso, cessare, cessavi, cessatum	I cease
ceterus -a -um	other, rest of
ceu	just as, like; as if (439)
cieo, ciere, civi, citum	I stir, rouse
*cingo, cingere, cinxi, cinctum	I strap on (511n.)
cinis, cineris *m.*	ash
circum (*adv.*)	all around
*circum + *acc.*	around
circumdo, circumdare, circumdedi, circumdatum + *dat.*	put around
circumfundo, circumfundere, circumfudi, circumfusum	I pour round; (*pass.*) I encircle (383n.)
circumspicio, circumspicere, circumspexi, circumspectum	I notice, discern
*civis, civis *m.*	citizen, townsperson
*clamor, clamoris *m.*	shout
clangor, clangoris *m.*	blaring, clanging (313)
claresco, clarescere, clarui	I become clear
claustrum -i *n.*	bolt, bar
clipeus -i *m.*	shield
*coepi, coepisse, coeptum (*defect.*)	I began
*cogo, cogere, coegi, coactum	I force; I coax out (196)
colligo, colligere, collegi, collectum	I gather together, muster
collum -i *n.*	neck
coluber, colubri *m.*	snake
columba, columbae *f.*	dove
coma -ae *f.*	hair

*comes, comitis *m.*	companion, comrade
comitor, comitari, comitatus sum	I accompany, attend
commendo, commendare, commendavi, commendatum	I entrust
compages, compagis *f.*	joint, fastening (51)
compello, compellare, compellavi, compellatum + *acc.*	I call to (280)
complector, complecti, complexus sum	I embrace
compleo, complere, complevi, completum	I fill up
composito (*adv.*)	by pre-arrangement (129)
comprimo, comprimere, compressi, compressum	I suppress, restrain
concedo, concedere, concessi, concessum	I withdraw
concido, concidere, concidi, concisum	I collapse
concilium -i *n.*	council
conclamo, conclamare, conclamavi, conclamatum	I clamour
concretus -a -um	matted (276)
concurro, concurrere, concurri, concursum	I charge (with others)
condensus -a -um	huddled together
*condo, condere, condidi, conditum	bury; (*pass.*) I hide myself (401)
configo, configere, confixi, confixum	I pierce
confligo, confligere, conflixi, conflictum	I collide

congredior, congredi, congressus sum	I converge; I clash (397)
conicio, conicere, conieci, coniectum	I hurl
coniunx, coniugis *c.*	spouse
consanguinitas, consanguinitatis *f.*	blood kinship
conscius -a -um + *gen.*	knowing of
consequor, consequi, consecutus sum	I follow
consero, conserere, conserui, consertum	I join
***consisto, consistere, constiti, constitum**	I halt, stand still
conspectus -us *m.*	view, sight
contexo, contexere, contexui, contextum	I weave; I form (112)
contingo, contingere, contigi, contactum	I touch
contorqueo, contorquere, contorsi, contorsum	I launch, propel
contra (*adv.*)	in opposition
convello, convellere, convelli, convulsum	I tear up
converto, convertere, converti, conversum	I turn, change
convolvo, convolvere, convolvi, convolutum	I turn around; I coil (474)
coram (*adv.*)	openly; before one's eyes (538)
Coroebus -i *m.*	Coroebus (386)
***corpus, corporis** *n.*	body, corpse

***corripio, corripere, corripui, correptum**	I seize, carry off
coruscus -a -um	dazzling, glinting
creber, crebra, crebrum	repeated
***credo, credere, credidi, creditum** + *dat.*	I believe, trust
cresco, crescere, crevi, cretum	I grow; I descend from (74)
***crimen, criminis** *n.*	accusation; wrongdoing (65)
crinis, crinis *m.*	hair
***crudelis -e**	cruel
cruentus -a -um	blood-stained
culmen, culminis *n.*	highest point (290); roof (446)
***culpa -ae** *f.*	blame, guilt
***cum** (*conj.*)	when, since
cum primum	as soon as
***cum** (*or* **-cum**) + *abl.*	with
cumulus -i *m.*	surge
***cunctus -a -um**	every, all
***cupio, cupere, cupivi/ -ii, cupitum**	I desire
***curo, curare, curavi, curatum**	I tend (536)
cursus -um *m.*	course, route
curvus -a -um	curved, arched
cuspes, cuspidis *f.*	spear-tip
***custos, custodis** *m.*	guard
Danai -orum *m. pl.*	descendants of Danaus (= Greeks)
Dardanidae -arum *m. pl.*	descendants of Dardanus (= Trojans)
***de** + *abl*	about; down from
***dea -ae** *f.*	goddess

*debeo, debere, debui, debitum	I owe
decem (*indecl.*)	ten
decorus -a -um	elegant, fine
decurro, decurrere, decurri/ decucurri, decursum	I run down
decus, decoris *n.*	honour, high repute
*defendo, defendere, defendi, defensum	I defend, protect
defensor, defensoris *m.*	defender
*defessus -a -um	tired
deficio, deficere, defeci, defectum	I lack; I am absent (505)
degener (*gen.* degeneris)	ignoble
Deiphobus -i *m.*	Deiphobus (311n.)
delabor, delabi, delapsus sum	I fall down; I stray (377)
delitesco, delitescere, delitui	I lie hidden
delubrum -i *n.*	citadel
demens (*gen.* dementis)	rash, foolish
demitto, demittere, demisi, demissum	I send down (398)
*denique	at last; eventually (295)
densus -a -um	close-packed
depascor, depasci, depastus sum	I feed on
depono, deponere, deposui, depositum	I put down, lay aside
destino, destinare, destinavi, destinatum	I appoint, nominate (129)
desuetus -a -um	disused
desuper (*adv.*)	from above
*deus -i *m.*	god

devolvo, devolvere, devolvi, devolutum	I roll down
dexter, dextra, dextrum	favourable (388)
***dextra -ae** f.*	right hand, arm
dictum -i *n.*	word
***dies, diei** *m. or f.*	day (132n.)
diffugio, diffugere, diffugi	I disperse, scatter
digero, digerere, digessi, digestum	I interpret, explain
***dignus -a -um** + *abl.*	worthy of
***discedo, discedere, discessi, discessum**	I depart
***disco, discere, didici**	I learn
discors (*gen.* **discordis**)	incongruous
***diu** (*adv.*)	for a long time
divello, divellere, divulsi, divulsum	I separate
diversus -a -um	various
***divido, dividere, divisi, divisum**	I break through (234)
divus -a -um	divine
***do, dare, dedi, datum**	I give
Dolopes, Dolopum *m. pl.*	Thessalians (= Greeks, 415n.)
***dolus -i** *m.*	treachery, deceit
domo, domare, domui, domitum	I subdue
***domus -us** f.	home
donec	until
***donum -i** *n.*	gift; sacrificial offering (49)
draco, draconis *m.*	snake
***dubius -a -um**	uncertain
***duco, ducere, duxi, ductum**	I lead; I draw (200, 288)

dulcis -e	sweet, dear
*dum	while, so long as; until (136)
duo, duae, duo	two
*durus -a -um	stout, tough
Dymas, Dymantis *m.*	Dymas (394)
*e/ex + *abl.*	from, out of
ecce	look! (57n., 402n.)
edissero, edissere, edisserui, edissertum	I explain fully
educo, educere, eduxi, eductum	I lead out; I extend (461)
effero, efferre, extuli, elatum	I bring out, draw out
effigies, effigiei *f.*	statue
effor, effari, effatus sum	I speak
effugium -i *n.*	escape
effundo, effundere, effudi, effusum	I pour out, shed
egeo, egere, egui + *abl.*	I lack, want
*ego, mei	I
elabor, elabi, elapsus sum	I slip away, escape
emico, emicare, emicui, emicatum	I spring up
emoveo, emovere, emovi, emotum	I dislodge (493)
*enim	for
ensis, ensis *m.*	sword
*eo, ire, ii/ivi	I go
Eous -a -um	of Eos, the dawn
equidem	indeed, truly
*equus -i *m.*	horse
*ergo	therefore

eripio, eripere, eripui, ereptum
+ *dat.*   I snatch away (134n.)

error, erroris *m.*   mistake, problem; threat (48)

erubesco, erubescere, erubui   I blush; respect (542)

*et   and

*etiam   also, even

Eurus -i *m.*   the south-easterly wind
     (417n.)

Eurypylus -i *m.*   Eurypylus (114)

evado, evadere, evasi, evasum   I go out, escape

evinco, evincere, evici, evictum   I overwhelm (497)

excindo, excindere, excidi,
excisum   I cut out

exclamo, exclamare, exclamavi,
exclamatum   I yell

excutio, excutere, excussi,
excussum   I shake out

exeo, exire, exii/ivi, exitum   I go out, escape

*exercitus -us *m.*   army

*exitium -i *n.*   death (131); disaster (190)

exitus -us *m.*   outcome, end

exoptatus -a -um   longed-for

exorior, exoriri, exortus sum   I arise

expendo, expendere, expendi,
expensum   I pay

expromo, expromere,
exprompsi, expromptum   I offer up (280)

exsanguis -e   pale (212); lifeless (542)

exscindo, exscindere, exscidi,
excissum   I uproot, destroy (177)

*exspecto, exspectare,
expectavi, exspectatum   I await

exsulto, exsultare, exsultavi, exsultatum	I revel
extemplo (*adv.*)	straightaway
extremus -a -um	final, last
exuo, exuere, exui, exutum	I strip
exuviae -arum *f. pl.*	spoils of war
fabrico, fabricare, fabricavi, fabricatum	I make, construct
facies, faciei *f.*	appearance
***facio, facere, feci, factum**	I make, do
factum -i *n.*	deed
falsus -a -um	untrue
***fama -ae** *f.*	report (82); rumour
fas (*indecl.*)	what is morally permissible (157n.)
fastigium -i *n.*	roof gable
fatalis -e	fateful (165); fatal (237)
fatum -i *n.*	destiny, fate
femineus -a -um	of women
fenestra -ae *f.*	window
ferio, ferire (*defect.*)	I strike
***fero, ferre, tuli, latum**	I bring, bear; I say (161, 230); I plunder (374); (*pass.*) I rush on (498, 511)
***ferrum -i** *n.*	sword, weaponry; tool (463)
ferus -i *m.*	beast
fessus -a -um	tired
***festino, festinare, festinavi, festinatum**	I hurry
festus -a -um	of a festival
fetus -a -um	pregnant; filled (238)

*fides, ei *f*.*	good faith, assurance; trustworthiness (309)
fido, fidere, fisus sum + *dat.*	I put trust in
fiducia -ae *f*.	trust, reliance
fidus -a -um	faithful
figo, figere, fixi, fixum	I affix (490)
fingo, fingere, finxi, fictum	I form, compose (107)
*finis, finis *m*.*	end
fio, fieri, factus sum	I become, happen
firmus -a -um	solid, strong
flagito, flagitare, flagitavi, flagitatum	I demand
*flamma -ae *f*.*	flame
fleo, flere, flevi, fletum	I weep
fluctus -us *m*.	wave
*flumen, fluminis *n*.*	river
fluo, fluere, fluxi	I ebb away (169)
foedo, foedare, foedavi, foedatum	I destroy, defile
for, fari, fatus sum	I speak, pronounce
foris, foris *f*.	door
formido, formidinis *f*.	fear
fors, fortis *f*.	chance, fortune
forsitan (*adv.*)	perhaps
*forte (*adv.*)*	by chance
Fortuna -ae *f*.	Fortuna, Fortune
frango, frangere, fregi, fractum	I shatter
fretum -i *n*.	strait
frigidus -a -um	cold
frons, frondis *f*.	leaf, foliage
frustra	in vain

frux, frugis *f.*	grain, produce
***fuga -ae** *f.*	flight, escape
***fugio, fugere, fugi**	I flee
***fundo, fundere, fudi, fusum**	I pour out (532); scatter, rout (421)
fundus -i *m.*	bottom, depth
funis, funis *m.*	rope
funus, funeris *n.*	death
furio, furiare, furiavi, furiatum	I enrage
furo, furere, furui	I rage
***furor, furoris** *m.*	fury (244n.)
***gaudeo, gaudere, gavisus sum**	I rejoice
gelidus -a -um	ice-cold
geminus -a -um	twin
gemitus -us *m.*	groan, sigh
genitor, genitoris *m.*	father
***gens, gentis** *f.*	people, race
***genus, generis** *n.*	kind, type
***gero, gerere, gessi, gestum**	I carry out; I exhibit (278)
glomero, glomerare, glomeravi, glomeratum	I assemble
gloria -ae *f.*	glory, renown
gradus -us *m.*	step; ladder rung (443)
Graius -a -um	Greek
gramen, graminis *n.*	grass, herb
grates (*nom. and acc. only*) *f. pl.*	thanks
gratus -a -um	welcome
***gravis -e**	heavy, serious
gurges, gurgitis *m.*	whirlpool
***habeo, habere, habui, habitum**	I have, hold; I deem (102)
haereo, haerere, haesi, haesum	I grip, cling

****hasta -ae** *f.*	spear
****haud**	not
Hector, Hectoris *m.*	Hector
Hectoreus -a -um	of Hector
Hecuba -ae *f.*	Hecuba (501n.)
heu	ah!
****hic** (*adv.*)	here; at this moment (122, 199)
****hic, haec, hoc**	this
****hiems, hiemis** *f.*	winter; storm
****hinc**	from here; from now (97n.)
****homo, hominis** *m.*	man
horrendus -a -um	bloodcurdling
horresco, horrescere, horrui	I start to shudder
****hortor, hortari, hortatus sum**	I encourage
hostia -ae *f.*	sacrifice
****hostis, hostis** *m.*	enemy
huc	to here
****humus -i** *f.*	ground
humi	on the ground
Hypanis, Hypanis *m.*	Hypanis (428)
****iaceo, iacere, iacui, iacitum**	I lie down
iacto, iactare, iactavi, iactatum	I sling, cast
iaculor, iaculari, iaculatus sum	I hurl
****iam**	now, by now, already
iamdudum	without delay (103n.)
ianua -ae *f.*	door
****ibi**	there
ictus -us *m.*	impact
ignarus -a -um	unaware
****ignis -is** *m.*	fire

ignotus -a -um	not known
Iliacus -a -um	of Ilium (= Trojan)
ilicet	immediately; at the last (424n.)
Ilium -i n.	Troy (117n.)
***ille, illa, illud**	that
imbellis -e	unfit for war
immanis -e	enormous
immemor (*gen.* **immemoris**) + *gen.*	oblivious to
immensus -a -um	vast
immisceo, immiscere, immiscui, immixtum	I mingle
immitto, immittere, immisi, immissum	I send forward (495)
impello, impellere, impuli, impulsum	I compel, force
***imperium -i** *n.*	power; domain
***impetus -us** *m.*	attack; hostility (74)
impius -a -um	godless
implico, implicare, implicui	I clasp
improbus -a -um	cruel, unjust
improvidus -a -um	unsuspecting
improvisus -a -um	unanticipated
imus -a -um	deepest
***in** + *acc.*	into, onto; towards (61); against (46); for the purpose of (131)
***in** + *abl.*	in, on
***incendo, incendere, incendi, incensum**	I set alight
incertus -a -um	hesitant, doubtful
incido, incidere, incidi	I fall upon (305); I fall on (467)

*incipio, incipere, incepi, inceptum	I begin
includo, includere, inclusi, inclusum	I shut in, enclose
inclutus -a -um	famous
incolumis -e	intact; unchallenged (88)
incomitatus -a -um	unaccompanied
incumbo, incumbere, incubui, incubitum + *dat.*	I lean on
incurro, incurrere, incurri, incursum	I charge in (409)
*inde	from then, from there
indicium -i *n.*	accusation, charge
indignor, indignari, indignatus sum	I grow indignant, resent
indignus -a -um + *abl.*	unfair, unmerited (285)
indomitus -a -um	unbridled, rampant
induo, induere, indui, indutum	I put on
inermis -e	unarmed
infandus -a -um	unspeakable, vile
infelix (*gen.* infelicis)	unlucky, unhappy
infensus -a -um	hostile
infestus -a -um	threatening
infula -ae *f.*	sacred headband
*ingens (*gen.* ingentis)	huge
ingratus -a -um	sorry, unwelcome
ingruo, ingruere, ingrui	I rush forward
inicio, inicere, inieci, iniectum	I throw forward (408)
inlabor, inlabi, inlapsus sum	I glide forward
inludo, inludere, inlusi, inlusum + *dat.*	I mock
innuptus -a -um	unmarried

*inquam, inquit	I say, he/she/it says *or* said
inritus -a -um	ineffectual, futile
inruo, inruere, inrui	I charge forward
insania -ae *f.*	madness
inscius -a -um	unaware
insequor, insequi, insecutus sum	I pursue
*insidiae -arum *f. pl.*	ambush, trap
insigne, insignis *n.*	distinctive mark; blazon (392)
insinuo, insinuare, insinuavi, insinuatum	I infiltrate
insono, insonare, insonui, insonitum	I ring out, clang
insons (*gen.* insontis)	blameless
inspicio, inspicere, inspexi, inspectum	I inspect, pry on
instauro, instaurare, instauravi, instauratum	I restore
insto, instare, insteti, instatum	I press forward
*instruo, instruere, instruxi, instructum	I prepare (152), arrange
intemeratus -a -um	untainted, undefiled
intendo, intendere, intendi, intensum	I stretch round
inter + *acc.*	among
intercludo, intercludere, interclusi, interclusum	I shut off, prohibit
*interea	meanwhile
interior, interius (*comparative adj.*)	inner
intus (*adv.*)	inside
inutilis -e	pointless, ineffectual

invado, invadere, invadi, invasum	I attack
inventor, inventoris *m.*	originator
invidium -i *n.*	jealousy
***invitus -a -um**	unwilling, reluctant
Iphitas, Iphitae *m.*	Iphitas (435n.)
***ipse, ipsa, ipsum**	himself, herself, itself (*emphatic*)
***ira -ae** *f.*	anger
***is, ea, id**	he, she, it
iste, ista, istud	that
***ita**	so, in this way
Ithacus -a -um	of Ithaca
iuba -ae *f.*	crest
***iubeo, iubere, iussi, iussum**	I order
iunctura -ae *f.*	joint
ius, iuris *n.*	oath
iussus -us *m.*	command
***iustus -a -um**	honourable, just
iuvenalis -e	of youth
***iuvenis, iuvenis** *m.*	young man
iuventa, ae *f.*	youthfulness
iuventus -us *f.*	youth; (*collective*) the young men
iuventus, iuventutis *f.*	group of young men
iuxta (*adv.*)	nearby
labes, labis *f.*	stain, blotch (97n.)
labo, labare, labavi, labatum	I totter, buckle
***labor, labi, lapsus sum**	I slip, fall
***labor, laboris** *m.*	work, toil; suffering (143)
***lacrima -ae** *f.*	tear
lacus -us *m.*	lake
***laedo, laedere, laesi, laesum**	I harm, offend

*laetus -a -um	happy
laeva -ae *f.*	left hand, arm
laevus -a -um	unfavourable (54)
lambo, lambere, lambi, lambitum	I lick
Laocoon, Laocoontos *m.*	Laocoon (41, 201nn.)
lapsus -us *m.*	sliding, slithering (225)
largus -a -um	copious
Larisaeus -a -um	of Larissa (197n.)
latebra -ae f.	hiding place
lateo, latere, latui	I lie hidden
latus -a -um	wide
late (*adv.*)	far and wide
latus, lateris *n.*	side, flank
laurus -i *f.*	laurel tree
*lego, legere, legi, lectum	I choose, pick
letum -i *n.*	death, destruction
levo, levare, levavi, levatum	I relieve, remove
*lex, legis *f.*	law
lignum -i *n.*	timber, woodwork
ligo, ligare, ligavi, ligatum	I bind, constrict
limen, liminis *n.*	threshold, entrance
limosus -a -um	muddy, slimy
lingua -ae *f.*	tongue
lito, litare, litavi, litatum	I seek divine favour
*litus, litoris *n.*	shore
loca -orum *n. pl.*	places, spaces
loco, locare, locavi, locatum	I put, position
*locum -i *n.*	place (495n.)
longaevus -a -um	old
*longus -a -um	long, extensive
*loquor, loqui, locutus sum	I speak
lorum -i *n.*	strip, thong

lubricus -a -um	glossy, moist
luctus -us *m.*	grief
lugeo, lugere, luxi, luctum	I mourn
lumen, luminis *n.*	light; life (85); eye (173, 405, 406)
lustro, lustrare, lustravi, lustratum	I survey
*****lux, lucis** *f.*	light, gleam
machina -ae *f.*	contraption, device
macto, mactare, mactavi, mactatum	I slaughter; I sacrifice (202)
maestus -a -um	sad, woeful
*****magis** (*adv.*)	more
*****magnus -a -um**	great
*****malus -a -um**	evil; toxic (471n.)
malum -i *n.*	evil, disaster (97)
*****maneo, manere, mansi, mansum**	I remain, endure
manica -ae *f.*	manacle
manifestus -a -um	evident
*****manus -us** *f.*	hand; handful of people
Mars, Martis *m.*	Mars
*****mater, matris** *m.*	mother
*****medius -a -um**	central, middle of
memini, meminisse (*defect.*)	I remember
memoro, memorare, memoravi, memoratum	I tell, recall
mendax (*gen.* **mendacis**)	deceitful, lying
*****mens, mentis** *f.*	thinking (316); mind, mindset (406)
mentior, mentiri, mentitus sum	I deceive (422); I falsely claim (540)

mercor, mercari, mercatus sum	I buy, trade
mereo, merere, merui, meritum	I earn, deserve
***meus -a -um**	my
mico, micare, micui	I glint; I flicker (475)
***miles, militis** *m.*	soldier; military
mille (*indecl.*)	a thousand
Minerva -ae *f.*	Minerva (= Athena)
minister, ministri *m.*	agent, attendant
***minor, minari, minatus sum** + *dat.*	I threaten
***mirabilis -e**	astonishing, miraculous
misceo, miscere, miscui, mixtum	I mix; I beset (298, 487)
***miser, misera, miserum**	poor, desperate
misereor, misereri, miseritus sum + *gen.*	I pity
miseresco, miserescere	I begin to pity
***mitto, mittere, misi, missum**	I send
***modo** (*adv.*)	only
***moenia -orum** *n. pl.*	city walls (234n.)
moles, is *f.*	huge structure (150, 185); earthwork (497)
molior, moliri, molitus sum	I undertake
***monstro, monstrare, monstravi, monstratum**	I show, indicate
monstrum -i *n.*	sign (171); monstrosity (245)
montanus -a -um	of a mountain
***mora -ae** *f.*	delay
***morior, mori, mortuus sum**	I die
***moror, morari, moratus sum**	I delay; I bother (102)
***mors, mortis** *f.*	death
morsus -us *m.*	bite

mortalis -e	mortal
mucro, mucronis *m.*	sword
mugitus -us *m.*	mooing
*__multus -a -um__	much, many
*__murus -i__ *m.*	wall
*__muto, mutare, mutavi,__ **mutatum**	I change
Mycenae -arum *f. pl.*	Mycenae (180, 192nn.)
*__nam__	for
namque	for indeed (67)
*__narro, narrare, narravi,__ **narratum**	I report, relate
nata -ae *f.*	daughter
natus -i *m.*	child; son
*__navis, navis__ *f.*	ship
ne + *infinitive*	do not (48n.)
*__ne__ + *subjunctive*	so that . . . not, lest
*__nec__	see **neque**
nefandus -a -um	wicked, abominable
nefas (*indecl.*)	what is not morally permissable (157n.)
*__nego, negare, negavi, negatum__	I deny, say . . . not
Neoptolemus -i *m.*	Neoptolemus (469n.)
nepos, nepotis *m.*	descendant
*__neque__ or **nec**	and not, nor
nec/neque . . . nec/neque . . .	neither . . . not
nequiquam	in vain
Nereus -i *m.*	Nereus (419n.)
nex, necis *f.*	death, slaughter
ni	if not, unless (178n.)
*__nihil__	nothing

nimbus -i *m.*	cloud
nitidus -a -um	lustrous, shiny
nitor, niti, nixus sum	I press on (380); I strain, strive (443)
nodus -i *m.*	knot
***nomen, nominis** *n.*	name
***non**	not
***nos, nostri/nostrum**	we, us
***noster, nostra, nostrum**	our
***notus -a -um**	known, famous
Notus -i *m.*	the southerly wind (417n.)
***novus -a -um**	new
***nox, noctis** *f.*	night
nudus -a -um	bare
numen, numinis *n.*	divine presence, god (141, 183); divine will, inclination (123, 233)
***numerus -i** *m.*	number
***nunc**	now
***nuntius -i** *m.*	messenger
nurus -us *f.*	daughter-in-law, daughter
nusquam	nowhere
o (*interjection*)	O
***ob** + *acc.*	because of
obicio, obicere, obieci, obiectum + *dat.*	I put in the way (444); (*pass.*) I befall (200)
***obliviscor, oblivisci, oblitus sum** + *gen.*	forget
obruo, obruere, obrui, obrutum	I attack, overwhelm
obscurus -a -um	dark, shady; hidden

*obsideo, obsidere, obsedi, obsessum	I besiege; I station myself (450n.)
obstupesco, obstupescere, obstipui	I am astonished
obtego, obtegere, obtexi, obtectum	I cover over, conceal
occasus -us *m.*	downfall, demise
occulto, occultare, occultavi, occultatum	I hide away
occumbo, occumbere, occubui, occubitum	I fall down
occumbo morti	I meet death (62)
*oculus -i *m.*	eye
*odi, odisse (*defect.*)	I hate
*odium -i *n.*	hatred, spite
*offero, offerre, obtuli, oblatum	I offer, present
omen, ominis *n.*	omen
*omnis -e	all, every
oppono, opponere, opposui, oppositum	I put in the way
oppono morti + *acc.*	I sentence to death someone (*acc.*) (127)
*opus, operis *n.*	task
*ora -ae *f.*	shore
oraculum -i *m.*	oracle
orbis, orbis *m.*	coil
Orcus -i *m.*	Orcus (397n.)
*ordo, ordinis *m.*	class, rank; category
*oro, orare, oravi, oratum	I beg
*os, oris *n.*	mouth (525), lips (246); face (530)
os, ossis *n.*	bone
osculum -i *n.*	kiss

Palamedes, Palamedis *m.*	Palamedes (82n.)
Palladium -i *n.*	the Palladium (166n.)
Pallas, Palladis *f.*	Pallas Athena (163n.)
palma -ae *f.*	hand, palm
pando, pandere, pandi, passum	I open up
Panthus, -i *m.*	Panthus (296n.)
paratus -a -um	ready
parco, parcere, peperci, parsum + *dat.*	I spare
parens, parentis *c.*	parent
***pareo, parere, parui, paritum** + *dat.*	I spare
paries, parietis *m.*	domestic wall
pariter (*adv.*)	together
parma -ae *f.*	small shield
***paro, parare, paravi, paratum**	I prepare
***pars, partis** *f.*	part
***parvus -a -um**	small
pascor, pasci, pastus sum	I consume
***passim** (*adv.*)	in every direction
pastor, pastoris *m.*	herdsman
***pater, patris** *m.*	father
patesco, patescere, patui	I become clear
***patria -ae** *f.*	fatherland
patrius -a -um	of a father (539); of one's homeland (279)
***pauper** (*gen.* **pauperis**)	poor
pavidus -a -um	alarmed, panicked
pavito, pavitare, pavitavi, pavitatum	I tremble in fear
pavor, pavoris *m.*	alarm, panic
pectus, pectoris *n.*	chest, breast

pelagus -i *n.*	sea
Pelasgi -orum *m. pl.*	the Pelasgi (= Greeks)
Pelasgus -a -um	Pelasgian (= Greek)
Pelias, Peliae *m.*	Pelias (435n.)
Pelides -ae *m.*	Achilles (548n.)
pellax (*gen.* **pellacis**)	deceitful
Pelopeus -a -um	of Pelops (= Greek)
penates, penatium *m. pl.*	Penates (293n.)
pendo, pendere, pependi, pensum	I hang from
Peneleus -i *m.*	Peneleus (425n.)
penetralia, penetralium *n. pl.*	innermost quarters
penitus (*adv.*)	deep within
per + *acc.*	through; all through; by (141n.)
pereo, perire, perii/perivi, peritum	I die
pererro, pererrare, pererravi, pererratum	I roam
perfundo, perfundere, perfudi, perfusus	I drench
Pergama, -orum *n. pl.*	Pergama (41n.)
Periphas, Periphantis *m.*	Periphas (476n.)
periurus -a -um	perjuring
perrumpo, perrumpere, perrupi, perruptum	I bust through
persolvo, persolvere, persolvi, persolutum	I pay
pervenio, pervenire, perveni, perventum	I reach
pervius -a -um	giving through-access (453)
pes, pedis *m.*	foot
peto, petere, petivi, petitum	I seek, attack
Phoebus -i *m.*	Apollo (114n.)

Phrygius -a -um	of Phrygia (= Trojan)
Phyrges, Phyrgum *m. pl.*	the Phrygians (= Trojans)
pietas, pietatis *f.*	duty to gods, family and fatherland
pio, piare, piavi, piatum	I expiate
placo, placare, placavi, placatum	I placate
plangor, plangoris *m.*	cry, lament
plurimus -a -um	very much, very many
***poena -ae** *f.*	punishment
Polites, -ae *m.*	Polites (526n.)
pone (*adv.*)	behind
***pono, ponere, posui, positum**	I put, place
pontus -i *m.*	sea
***populus -i** *m.*	people, population
***porta -ae** *f.*	gate
porticus -us *m.*	colonnade
***posco, poscere, poposci**	I demand
***possum, posse, potui**	I am able
***post** + *acc.*	behind; after
postis -is *m.*	door-post
***postquam** (*conj.*)	after
***potens** (*gen.* **potentis**)	powerful
praeceps (*gen.* **praecipitis**)	headlong (307n.); steeply-descending (460n.)
praecipito, praecipitare, praecipitavi, praecipitatum	I rush
praecipue (*adv.*)	especially
***praemium -i** *n.*	reward
premo, premere, pressi, pressum	I push down, tread on
prendo, prendere, prendi, prensum	I grasp

Priameius -a -um	born to Priam
Priamus -i *m.*	Priam (484n.)
primum	at first
***primus -a -um**	first
***prius** (*comparative adv.*)	first, sooner
***pro** + *abl.*	in the place of; on behalf of
***procul** (*adv.*)	from afar, far off
procumbo, procumbere, procubui, procubitum	I fall forward
proditio, proditionis *f.*	betrayal; trumped-up charge (83)
***prodo, prodere, prodidi, proditum**	I betray
***proelium -i** *n.*	battle, skirmish
***promitto, promittere, promisi, promissum**	I promise, pledge
propinquus -a -um	related by family (86)
prosequor, prosequi, prosecutus sum	I continue on (106)
protego, protegere, protexi, protectum	I protect
protinus (*adv.*)	straightaway
protraho, protrahere, protraxi, protractum	I lead forward, lead out
***proximus -a -um**	very near, neighbouring
pubes, pubis *f.*	youth, young men
***puella -ae** *f.*	girl
***puer, pueri** *m.*	boy
***pugna -ae** *f.*	fight
***pulcher, pulchra, pulchrum**	beautiful, handsome
pulvis, pulveris *m.*	dust
puppis, puppis *f.*	stern; ship (276)

*puto, putare, putavi, putatum   I think, consider
Pyrrhus -i *m.*   Pyrrhus (469n.)

qua (*adv.*)   where (455n.)
*quaero, quaerere, quaesivi,   I seek, ask
    quaesitum
*qualis -e   of what sort
*quamquam   although
*quando   when?
quantum (*adv.*)   how much
quater (*adv.*)   four times
*-que   and
*qui, quae, quod   who, which
*qui, quae, quod (*interrogative*   which? what?
    adj.)
qui, qua, quod (*indefinite adj.*)   any (94, 141)
*quia   since
quicumque, quaecumque,   whoever, whatever
    quodcumque
quid?   why?
*quies, quietis *f.*   rest, sleep
quinquaginta (*indecl.*)   fifty
quinus -a -um   five (each)
quis, quid   who? what?; any (420n.)
*quisque, quidque   each person, each thing
*quisquis, quidquid   whoever, whatever
*quo (*adv.*)   to where? (520), to what end?
        (150)

quondam   at one time, formerly

rapidus -a -um   swift, rushing
rapio, rapere, rapui, raptum   I take, I seize

rapto, raptare, raptavi, raptatum	I drag violently
***ratio, rationis** f.*	reason, rationale
raucus -a -um	clanging
recedo, recedere, recessi, recessum	I stand back
***recens** (*gen.* **recentis**)	fresh, recent
***recipio, recipere, recepi, receptum**	I receive
recuso, recusare, recusavi, recusatum	I refuse
recutio, recutere, recussi, recussum	I reverberate (52)
***reddo, reddere, reddidi, redditum**	I hand over
***redeo, redire, redii/ivi, reditum**	I return
reditus -us *m.*	return
***reduco, reducere, reduxi, reductum**	I lead back
***refero, referre, rettuli, relatum**	I bring back
refugio, refugere, refugi	I retreat
regnator, regnatoris *m.*	ruler
***regnum -i** *n.*	kingdom, domain
religio, religionis *f.*	religious duty, observance (150n.); sanctity (188n.)
***relinquo, relinquere, reliqui, relictus**	I leave behind; I neglect (454)
reluceo, relucere, reluxi	I sparkle, gleam
remeo, remeare, remeavi, remeatum	I go back
remetior, remetiri, remensus sum	I retrace (181n.)

remitto, remittere, remisi, remissum	I send back
repello, repellere, reppuli, repulsum	I repel
rependo, rependere, rependi, repensum	I pay back
***repente** (*adv.*)*	suddenly
repeto, repetere, repetivi, repetitum	I seek again
reporto, reportare, reportavi, reportatum	I bring back, relay
reposco, reposcere	I demand back
reprimo, reprimere, repressi, repressum	I check, suppress
requiesco, requiescere, requievi, requietum	I rest
***res, rei** f.*	matter, thing; story, account (195)
resolvo, resolvere, resolvi, resolutum	I annul (157)
***responsum -i** n.*	answer
resto, restare, restiti	I remain
retro (*adv.*)	back, backwards
revincio, revincire, revinxi, revinctum	I tie back, bind
revolvo, revolvere, revolvi, revolutum	I go back over, dwell upon (101)
***rex, regis** m.*	king
Rhipheus -i *m.*	Rhipheus (394)
robur, roboris *n.*	oak; timber (186)
***rogo, rogare, rogavi, rogatum**	I ask
rota -ae *f.*	wheel

ruina -ae *f.*	ruin, destruction
***rumpo, rumpere, rupi, ruptum**	I break
***ruo, ruere, rui, ruitum**	I rush; collapse (290)
***rursus**	again
sacer, sacra, sacrum	sacred
sacratus -a -um	sanctified
***saepe**	often
saevio, saevire, saevii, saevitum	I seethe, rage
***saevus -a -um**	cruel
salsus -a -um	salted
***salus, salutis** *f.*	safety, survival
sanguineus -a -um	blood-red
***sanguis, sanguinis** *m.*	blood; family line (74)
sanies, saniei *f.*	gore
***sat(is)** (*indecl.*)	enough
sata -orum *n. pl.*	crops
saucius -a -um	wounded
saxum -i *n.*	rock
scala -ae *f.*	ladder
scando, scandere, scandi, scansum	I climb
sceleratus -a -um	sacrilegious
***scelus, sceleris** *n.*	crime, wickedness
scitor, scitari, scitatus sum	I ask (105n.)
Scyrius -a -um	of Scyros (477n.)
***se** (*or* **sese**)	himself, herself, itself, themselves (*reflexive*)
secretus -a -um	set apart
securis, securis *f.*	axe
secus (*adv.*)	otherwise

***sedes, sedis** f.	seat; abode
seges, segetis f.	crop-field; crop
segnities, segnitiei f.	inertia
***semper**	always
senior, senius (*comparative adj.*)	rather old
***sentio, sentire, sensi, sensum**	I realize
sentis, sentis m.	thicket
sepulcrum -i n.	tomb, burial
serenus -a -um	calm, clear
sero, serere, sevi, satum	I beget
serpens, serpentis c.	snake
serpo, serpere, serpsi, serptum	I slither
serus -a -um	late; delaying (374)
***servo, servare, servavi, servatum**	preserve, protect; attend to (427n.)
seu/ sive	if either
***si**	if
sibilus -a -um	hissing
***sic**	so, in this way
sidus, sideris n.	star
Sigeus -a -um	of Sigeum (312n.)
signo, signare, signavi, signatum	I note, register
***signum -i** n.	sign, signal
sileo, silere, silui	I am silent
***silva -ae** f.	wood
***simul**	at the same time; while (220)
simulacrum -i n.	icon, effigy
sin	but if
***sine** + *abl.*	without
***sinistra -ae** f.	left hand, arm
Sinon, Sinonis m.	Sinon

sinuo, sinuare, sinuavi, sinuatum	I bend, flex
sisto, sistere, stiti, statum	I set, position
socer, soceri *m.*	parent-in-law
socius -a -um	allied
socius -i *m.*	comrade
***sol, solis** *m.*	sun
***soleo, solere, solitus sum**	I am accustomed
sollemnis -e	customary
solum -i *n.*	soil, ground
somnus -i *m.*	sleep
sonitus -us *m.*	sound
sono, sonare, sonui, sonitum	I sound, resonate
***sonus -i** *m.*	sound
spargo, spargere, sparsi, sparsum	I sow, spread (98)
species, speciei *f.*	sight, appearance
***spes, spei** *f.*	hope
spira -ae *f.*	coil
***spolium -i** *n.*	spoil, war-trophy
spumo, spumare, spumavi, spumatum	I foam
squaleo, squalere, squalui	I am filthy
squameus- a- um	scaly
stabulum -i *n.*	stable, pen
***statuo, statuere, statui, statutum**	I set up, construct
sterno, sternere, stravi, stratum	I lay low, crush
***sto, stare, steti, statum**	I stand
strido, stridere, stridi	I shreak, howl
stringo, stringere, strinxi, strictum	I draw out, unsheathe
struo, struere, struxi, structum	I produce, accomplish

**studium -i *n.*	eagerness
stupeo, stupere, stupui	I am astonished
stuppeus -a -um	flaxen; towing (236)
*sub + *acc.*	up against (442); towards (460)
*sub + *abl.*	under
subeo, subire, subii/ivi, subitum + *dat.*	I come to
subicio, subicere, subieci, subiectum	I place under
sublabor, sublabi, sublapsus sum	I sink under (169)
subsisto, subsistere, substiti	I stop short (243)
succedo, succedere, successi, successum	I approach
successus -us *m.*	success
succurro, succurrere, succurri, succursum + *dat.*	I run towards; I occur (317)
suffero, sufferre, sustuli, sublatum	I withstand (492)
sufficio, sufficere, suffeci, suffectum	suffuse
*sum, esse, fui	I am
*summus -a -um	uppermost, top of
*sumo, sumere, sumpsi, sumptum	I take, exact
super (*adv.*)	moreover (71)
super + *abl.*	on top of (466)
superbus -a -um	proud
superi -orum *m. pl.*	gods
*supero, superare, superavi, superatum	I overcome; I overtop (207)
*superus -a -um	upper

supplex, supplicis *m./f.*	suppliant
suspensus -a -um	uncertain, doubtful (114)
tabulatum -i *n.*	floor, storey
taceo, tacere, tacui, tacitum	I am silent
*talis -e	of such a kind
*tamen	however
*tandem	at last
*tantus -a- um	so great, such great
tardus -a -um	impeded, delayed
taurus -i *m.*	bull
*tectum -i *n.*	roof (302, 461); palace (440n.)
*tego, tegere, texi, tectum	I cover; I hide away (126)
tellus, telluris *f.*	land, territory
*telum -i *n.*	weapon, spear, missile
*tempestas, tempestatis *f.*	storm
tempto, temptare, temptavi, temptatum	I venture
tempus, temporis *n.*	time, moment; (*pl.*) temples
tendo, tendere, tetendi, tensum	I seek (205); I attempt (220); I aim (405)
tenebrae -arum *f. pl.*	darkness
Tenedos -i *f.*	Tenedos (203n.)
*teneo, tenere, tenui, tentum	I keep (281)
tener, tenera, tenerum	soft, tender
tenus + *abl.*	all the way to
ter	three times
*tergum -i *n.*	back
*terra -ae *f.*	ground, territory
*terreo, terrere, terrui, territum	I frighten
testor, testari, testatus sum + *acc.*	I call upon, invoke

testudo, testudinis *f.*	shield-formation; siege weapon (441n.)
Teucri -orum *m. pl.*	Teucrians (= Trojans)
thalamus -i *m.*	bedroom
***timeo, timere, timui**	I fear
***tollo, tollere, sustuli, sublatum**	I raise, lift
torrens, torrentis *m.*	torrent
***totus -a -um**	whole
trabs, trabis *f.*	beam
***traho, trahere, traxi, tractum**	I drag, lead, bring (465); I eke out (92)
traicio, traicere, traieci, traiectum	I pierce
tranquillus -a -um	calm
tremefacio, tremefacere, tremefeci, tremefactum	I make tremble
tremo, tremere, tremui	I tremble; I dread (199)
tremor, tremoris *m.*	tremor
trepidus -a -um	fearful, frightened
***tristis -e**	woeful, sad
trisulcus -a -um	triple-forked
Tritonia -ae *f.*	Athena (171n.)
Tritonis, Tritonidis *f.*	Athena (226)
Troia -ae *f.*	Troy
Troianus -a -um	of Troy, Trojan
trucido, trucidare, trucidavi, trucidatum	I kill
truncus -i *m.*	torso
***tu, tui**	you (*sing.*)
tuba -ae *f.*	war-bugle
tueor, tueri, tuitus sum	I oversee, protect
***tum**	then

tumeo, tumere, tumui, tumitum	I swell
tumidus -a -um	swollen
***tumultus -us** *m.*	commotion
tunc	then
turbo, turbare, turbavi, turbatum	I agitate, disturb
turbo, turbinis *m.*	whirlwind
turpis -e	disgraceful, shameful
turris, turris *f.*	tower
***tuus -a -um**	your (*singular*)
Tydides, Tydidae *m.*	Diomedes (164m.)
Ucalegon, Ucalegontis *m.*	Ucalegon (311n.)
Ulixes, Ulixi *m.*	Ulysses (= Odysseus)
***ullus -a -um**	any
***ultimus -a -um**	last
ultor, ultoris *m.*	avenger
ultro (*adv.*)	by one's own initiative (59, 145); going further (192)
ululo, ululare, ululavi, ululatum	I wail (488)
ulva -ae *f.*	swamp-grass
umbo, umbonis *m.*	shield boss
umbra -ae *f.*	shade, shadow
umerus -i *m.*	shoulder
***umquam**	ever
***unde**	from where
***undique**	from all sides
unus -a -um	one
***urbs, urbis** *f.*	city
usquam	anywhere
***usus -us** *m.*	purpose, function, feature

ut (or uti) + indicative	as, when, how (283)
ut + subjunctive	that, so that
*uterque, utraque, utrumque	either (of two)
uterus -i *m.*	womb
utinam	if only
vacuus -a -um	empty
vado, vadere	I proceed
*valeo, valere, valui, valitum	I am able
*validus -a -um	strong
vanus -a -um	empty; destitute (80)
varius -a -um	various
vates, vatis *m.*	seer, prophet
*-ve	or
*vel	or
vello, vellere, velli, vulsum	I tear away
velo, velare, velavi, velatum	I deck, adorn
velum -i *n.*	sail
vela do	I set sail (136)
*velut(i)	just as, like
venenum -i *n.*	poison, venom
*venio, venire, veni, ventum	I come, arrive
*ventus -i *m.*	wind
*verbum -i *n.*	word
*vero	indeed
verso, versare, versavi, versatum	I turn over; I accomplish (62n.)
vertex, verticis *m.*	top, summit
*verus -a -um	true, real
verum, -i *n.*	the truth (141)
Vesta -ae *f.*	Vesta (296–7nn.)
*vester, vestra, vestrum	your (*pl.*)

vestibulum -i *n.*	front court
***veto, vetare, vetui, vetitum**	I avoid
***vetus** (*gen.* **veteris**)	old, ancient
***via -ae** *f.*	path, way
vibro, vibrare, vibravi,	I quiver, vibrate
vibratum	
vices (*defect.*) *f. pl.*	changes; hazards (433n.)
***victor, victoris** *m.*	victor
***video, videre, vidi, visum**	I see; (*pass.*) I seem
vigeo, vigere	I flourish, thrive
vinc(u)lum -i *n.*	chain (134); rope (236)
***vinco, vincere, vici, victum**	I defeat, conquer
violabilis -e	violable
violo, violare, violavi, violatum	I violate
***vir, viri** *m.*	man; husband
vis (*defect. – acc.* **vim,** *abl.* **vi**)	violence, force
vires, virium *f. pl.*	strength; forces
virgineus -a -um	maidenly
virgo, virginis *f.*	young unmarried woman
viso, visere, visi, visum	I observe, inspect
visus -us *m.*	sight
***vita -ae** *f.*	life
vito, vitare, vitavi, vitatum	I avoid
vitta -ae *f.*	woollen band (133n.); garland
***vix**	scarcely, hardly
***voco, vocare, vocavi, vocatum**	I summon, call
Volcanus -i *m.*	Vulcan (311n.)
***volo, velle, volui**	I want
volumen, voluminis *n.*	fold, coil
***vos, vestri/vestrum**	you (*pl.*)

*vox, vocis f.	voice, word
vulgus -i m.	mob (99n.)
*vulnus, vulneris n.	wound
*vultus -us m.	face, expression
Zephyrus -i m.	the west wind (417)